# SHORT FILM SCRIPTS


# Nikhil Kamkolkar

# SHORT FILM SCRIPTS

By Nikhil Kamkolkar

Identifiers

ISBN 978-1-970338-07-2 (paperback)

ISBN 978-1-970338-08-9 (hardcover)

# TABLE OF CONTENTS

Chapter One - How to Read a Screenplay ........................................................................ 1

Chapter Two - About "The Dark Between Us" .................................................................. 3

    THE DARK BETWEEN US ...................................................................................... 5

    HOLDEN ................................................................................................................... 17

    YOUR ONLY HOPE ................................................................................................. 27

Chapter Three - About "Le Nid" & "Leaving Priyanka" ............................................... 35

    THE NEST (LE NID) ............................................................................................... 36

    LEAVING PRIYANKA ............................................................................................ 47

Chapter Four - About "Sunflower/Soul" and "Tulip/Rock" ......................................... 56

    TULIP/ROCK ........................................................................................................... 58

    SUNFLOWER/SOUL ............................................................................................... 60

Chapter Five - About "Liberty" ..................................................................................... 66

    LIBERTY .................................................................................................................. 67

About the Author ........................................................................................................... 101

More From the Author ................................................................................................... 103

# Chapter One

## How to Read a Screenplay

Screenplays are a unique form of storytelling—part blueprint, part poetry. They ask the reader's imagination to fill in the gaps, just as a film crew will one day turn the words into images and sound.

A screenplay isn't a novel; it's a blueprint for a film. Scenes are introduced with headers (also called scene headings or slug lines) like:

```
INT. BEDROOM - NIGHT
```

"INT." (interior) means the action takes place indoors—here, in a bedroom. "NIGHT" indicates the time of day.

```
EXT. NEW JERSEY STREETS - DAY
```

"EXT." (exterior) means the action is outside. "Day" tells us it's daytime.

Descriptions are concise, focused on visible action and dialogue. Internal thoughts generally aren't written—that's for actors and directors to interpret. For example:

```
INT. BEDROOM - NIGHT

Jane turns and stares at the gun Jack aims at her heart.

                JANE
        Hello, Jack.

                JACK
        Hi, Jane.
```

Pretty spare on the page, right? Now picture Julia Roberts and Richard Gere performing it. Or Brad Pitt and Angelina Jolie. The magic happens when talented actors, directors, and crew breathe life into these words. As you read, bring your inner filmmaker to the table—imagine the emotions, performances, and visuals.

Sometimes you'll see "parentheticals," quick cues about delivery or tone. Here's the same scene with a couple added:

```
INT. BEDROOM - NIGHT

Jane turns and stares at the gun Jack has aimed at her
heart.

                    JANE
             (happy)
        Hello, Jack.

Beat.

                    JACK
             (cold)
        Hi, Jane.
```

Here, Jane is happy to see Jack, but he's cold toward her. Most actors I know (myself included) cross these out as they do their own analysis and make personal choices.

Still, parentheticals can help a script reader who doesn't have time for deep analysis grasp the intended tone.

Another word above—"Beat"—indicates a brief pause in the rhythm. It signals that something shifts: the character is processing, weighing, scheming—whatever the moment demands—before speaking. Use it sparingly. They sometimes serve more as reminder to me that there's a shift in the character's emotional thrust at this point.

Alright, with those basics under our belt, let's dive in!

# Chapter Two

## About "The Dark Between Us"

The journey of THE DARK BETWEEN US began with a script titled YOUR ONLY HOPE.

I wrote YOUR ONLY HOPE while my debut feature, the romantic comedy Love Love, was playing at a festival in Setúbal. The streets of Lisbon, the tranquility of Tróia, and my urge to write a dark thriller all seeped into the pages.

Over time, the story evolved, but its Portuguese inspirations stayed. In that first version, I named the protagonist HOLDEN—an homage to the iconic figure from The Catcher in the Rye, a book that left a lasting mark on me.

The next iteration, simply titled HOLDEN, shifted the story to New York City—a production-friendly choice since I lived and worked in the metro area.

We finally shot the film during the pandemic. That draft became THE DARK BETWEEN US, rewritten for two talented South Asian actors based in New York. Given the circumstances, we filmed in an actor's apartment, masked, with a tiny crew.

Even then, its Portuguese genesis persisted. The finished short includes ferry footage to Tróia that I shot of my wife and our then-infant daughter during a festival-organized tour.

THE DARK BETWEEN US went on to win a Best Creator award at the Seoul Webfest, earn a nomination for Best Suspense/Thriller, and place #5 on Coverfly's Thriller list.

Short films are where I experiment and grow as a storyteller. This project showed me how dramatically an idea can morph from spark to screen.

Below, you'll find all three versions: THE DARK BETWEEN US (an early draft of the produced film), HOLDEN (the noir NYC iteration), and YOUR ONLY HOPE (the earliest version).

I hope you enjoy reading the outcome of this long journey this project took.

# THE DARK BETWEEN US

**INT. KITCHEN - NIGHT**

CLOSE ON: A KNIFE cuts through the layers of AN ONION.

WE ARE IN a NEW YORK CITY apartment.

AMAR, Indian-American, 30s, pauses the cutting to look up towards the bedroom with an expression of sadness and anger.

He raises the hand with the knife to wipe his face.

PASTA WITH BROCCOLI boils on the stove.

>             AMAR
> Ruhi?

No response.

CLOSE ON KNIFE as Amar places it on the cutting board and heads towards the bedroom.

**INT. BEDROOM - NIGHT**

RUHI, indeterminate ethnicity, 30s, stands shrouded in darkness, staring out at the night view of the city. She doesn't turn when she hears Amar.

>             AMAR (O.S.)
> You must be hungry. You haven't
> eaten for two days.

Ruhi continues to stare at the city and speaks - almost to herself.

>             RUHI
> It was too good to be true.

Amar -- standing in the doorway. Too afraid to move closer.

>             AMAR
> The past is the past. We are here
> now. Just you and I.

>             RUHI
> You are married. And I had no idea.

                         AMAR
              I should have told you the truth.

Ruhi holds up a PHOTO FRAME. The PHOTO is hidden from us.

                         RUHI
              About your wife? About your other
              identity?

                         AMAR
              About everything. The real truth.

                         RUHI
              Will that make me happy? You
              promised to keep me happy. That was
              the deal.

Beat.

                         AMAR
              Let it go. And let's eat. Please.

She shoves the frame into his hands and leaves.

                         RUHI
              I'm done with you.

The front door slams shut.

                         AMAR
              Ruhi...

Amar looks at the frame for a moment. Throws it.


**INT. LIVING ROOM - NIGHT**

The frame lands on the sofa. Face down.


**INT. STAIRCASE - NIGHT**

Ruhi runs up the stairs. Moments later, Amar follows.


**EXT. ROOFTOP - NIGHT**

Ruhi watches the night skyline of Manhattan lost in thought.
Amar comes up to her.

                         AMAR
              Don't leave, Ruhi.

>               RUHI
>     Will you keep me happy if I stay?

>               AMAR
>     I promise.

Ruhi regards him warily for a moment. Then --

>               RUHI
>     I'm hungry.

Amar smiles.

>               AMAR
>     I know.

A trance-y piece of MUSIC with a TABLA beat begins to play.

Ruhi walks back, Amar stares after her for a moment. Then follows her.

**INT. LIVING ROOM - NIGHT**

CLOSE ON: Ruhi dances - a slow, swaying dance. As if she's in a trance of some kind.

**INT. KITCHEN - NIGHT**

Amar -- washes PLATES in the sink as he watches her.

AMAR'S POV: Ruhi laughs and smiles as she sways to the music. She doesn't even LOOK at him.

Amar POURS wine in two glasses. He walks over to her. Hands her one. Raises his own in a toast.

>               AMAR
>     Tchin Tchin.

Ruhi takes the glass, DOWNS the wine, and hands it back.

>               AMAR
>     Happy?

A curious smile. Then, she shakes her head.

>               RUHI
>     Where is she?

>               AMAR
>     Who?

> RUHI
> The wife.

> AMAR
> I don't know. She left me.
> Remember?

> RUHI
> You never told me where she went?

> AMAR
> No, I didn't. Because I don't know
> where she went. Do we have to do
> this?

**INT. KITCHEN - NIGHT**

Amar moves into the kitchen. Pours his wine into the sink
with a pointed glare at her.

Ruhi moves across the counter and stands facing him.

> RUHI
> Why didn't you get a divorce?
> Convince me that everything you
> said about what happened is the
> truth.

> AMAR
> She disappeared. I couldn't get a
> divorce. So I changed my identity.
> Started a new life. Met you. Okay?

Amar starts to rinse the glasses --

> RUHI
> Something must have happened to
> her.

> AMAR
> Sure. Marriage. Kids. She always
> wanted kids.

> RUHI
> Something bad must have happened to
> her. And you are hiding it from me.

Amar walks over holding the knife he was washing.

**INT. LIVING ROOM - NIGHT**

>                AMAR
>      What do you want, Ruhi? What do you
>      want from me?

>                RUHI
>      Are you going to hurt me?

Amar realizes he's holding a knife and goes back into the
kitchen. Throws the knife in the sink.

>                AMAR
>      Go to hell.

**INT. BEDROOM - NIGHT**

Amar walks into the bedroom and stares out at the night city
view from the window. A mirror image of what Ruhi did
before.

>                RUHI (V.O.)
>      Did you hurt her?

**INT. LIVING ROOM - NIGHT**

Ruhi also stares out at the night city view -- but from the
window in the living room.

INTERCUT - LIVING ROOM / BEDROOM

>                RUHI
>      Did you hurt her?

>                AMAR
>      No.

>                RUHI
>      When did you see her last?

>                AMAR
>      I don't remember...

Ruhi -- confident.

>                RUHI
>      It was Lisbon.

>                AMAR
>      What?

                    RUHI
          The last time you saw her was in
          Lisbon. Portugal. June. Two years
          ago.

                    AMAR
          How do you know...?

                    RUHI
          I know. You can't hide anything
          from me, Amar.

                    AMAR
          You are right. I remember now. It
          was Lisbon. I had convinced her to
          go with me for our anniversary. One
          last chance to try and fix our
          marriage...
               (beat)
          On our last day there, she insisted
          on going to a concert in a park by
          some musician who was a national
          treasure of Portugal or some such
          bullshit. It was a beautiful day.
          She looked so radiant in the
          sunlight. Laughing and smiling and
          dancing. She never once looked at
          me. Like I wasn't even there.

Amar -- lost in the memory.

                    RUHI
          And then?

                    AMAR
          Then?
               (shrugs)
          We got back to the hotel. She
          packed her bags and left.

Ruhi appears in the doorway.

                    RUHI
          And that's the truth?

                    AMAR
          Yes.

                    RUHI
          Amar, she never made it back to the
          hotel.

She walks closer to him - coming face-to-face.

>                    AMAR
>           What do you mean?

>                    RUHI
>           She was watching the sunset...

>                    AMAR
>           What sunset?

>                    RUHI
>           The sunset over the Arrabida
>           mountain.

>                    AMAR
>           Take your goddamn meds, Ruhi.
>           There's no way you can know that.

>                    RUHI
>           You talk in your sleep. You talk in
>           your sleep and you said you killed
>           her on the ferry back from Troia.
>           What happened on the ferry, Amar?
>           What did you do to her?

>                    AMAR
>           The ferry ride from Troia... Yes, I
>           remember now.

Ruhi watches him as he struggles to recall. But she could
swear he's struggling to lie, and watches him carefully.

>                    AMAR
>           After the concert, I convinced her
>           to go with me to Troia. Where we
>           had first met. Hoping it'd rekindle
>           happy memories. But she... she had
>           come with me only to exorcize every
>           last happy memory of us. And she
>           did that with a vengeance.
>                (beat)
>           On our way back from Troia, she
>           stood on the empty deck of the
>           ferry, smiling into the freezing
>           wind, happy at her freedom from me.
>           She told me it was over and walked
>           away. I stood there for a long
>           time. Frozen in tears...

**INT. BATHROOM - NIGHT**

Ruhi sits on the toilet. Face buried in her hands. Is she
crying? Can't tell.

                                                CUT TO:

Ruhi squats on the floor -- desperately searches for, then
pulls out a CIGARETTE PACK from her hiding spot in the
cabinet under the sink.

                                                CUT TO:

Ruhi looks at her face in the mirror, divided into two by
the seam in the glass as she places a cigarette in her lips
and lights it.

Then, she looks up at herself.

**INT. LIVING ROOM - NIGHT**

Amar sits on the sofa -- looking at the PHOTO FRAME. He
rises to face her -- still holding the frame.

                    AMAR
          Do you believe me?

                    RUHI
          Oh Amar. I don't know what to
          believe.

                    AMAR
               (confused)
          I don't know why I couldn't
          remember...

                    RUHI
          People process emotional trauma in
          different ways.

                    AMAR
          I'm just trying to put it all
          behind me...

                    RUHI
          I know, my love.

                    AMAR
          Do you believe me, Ruhi?

A moment as Ruhi considers.

                    RUHI
          I do.
               (beat)
          You and I, together, we will put it
          all behind us together. Do you
          trust me?

                    AMAR
          I do.

Ruhi and Amar kiss. Ruhi pulls herself away. Sits on the
sofa. She inhales and exhales.

                    RUHI
          We'll always be together now.

Amar looks at the PHOTO in the frame.

                    AMAR
          It's freezing cold.

Ruhi grabs a blanket from a basket on the floor.

                    RUHI
          Come, my love. I'll warm you up.

                    AMAR
          Ruhi...

                    RUHI
          Yes, my love?

                    AMAR
          She never got off the ferry.

                    RUHI
          Amar, don't play games with me.

                    AMAR
          Her body washed ashore on a Troia
          beach three days after I returned
          to the States.

Ruhi -- stunned by this admission. She recovers.

                    RUHI
          Amar, you promised to keep me
          happy.

                    AMAR
              (speaking rapidly now)
          She stood on the deck, all alone...
          and you were there, Ruhi. It wasn't
          me. It was you! You were there with
          her.

Ruhi screams and rises. Amar grabs her by the shoulder. They
are locked in a strong braced position.

                    RUHI
          STOP IT!

> AMAR
> She stood there alone...

> RUHI
> ...smiling into the freezing wind.

> AMAR
> Staring out at the sunset over the
> Arrabida mountain.

Ruhi, desperate now --

> RUHI
> Amar, please. Don't make me sad.

> AMAR
> Fado's music played in the
> background. And you hated it.

> RUHI
> But I still stood there next to
> her. Hoping she'd want me. But...

> AMAR
> ...she pushed you away with so much
> contempt.

> RUHI
> I felt it. I  felt her complete
> rejection of me.

> AMAR
> You tried to hold her hand.

> RUHI
> And she slapped me.

> AMAR
> ...You... got angry. And...

> RUHI
> ...I... pushed her...

Ruhi pushes Amar who stumbles backwards a couple of steps.
Ruhi turns away from him. Amar comes back and stands next to
her and both look out -- as if they are on the ferry.

> AMAR
> She went over the railing. I saw
> her hit the water.

> RUHI
> Her eyes, filled with such hate for
> me.

                    AMAR
          I wanted to jump into the water to
          save her...

                    RUHI
          But I didn't let you.

                    AMAR
          You pushed me back into the dark.
          I didn't do anything bad to her,
          Ruhi. You did.

Ruhi's face turns cold and angry. She turns away from him
and goes to grab her cigarette pack. Takes one out. Lights
it.

                    AMAR
          That's the real truth.

                    RUHI
          Shhh...

                    AMAR
          Accept it. And move on.

                    RUHI
          The only truth you need to know is
          that we had nothing to do with her
          death.

                    AMAR
          But we did. You did. You killed her
          because she didn't want to be your
          wife anymore. You couldn't deal
          with that. Don't you remember? Stop
          lying to yourself.

Ruhi and Amar stand face-to-face.

                    AMAR
          Please don't make it dark, Ruhi.
          You need the truth.

Ruhi looks at him with deep contempt. Her expression is hard
and cold.

                    RUHI
          I need you to lie. You are no good
          to me if you can't.

Ruhi takes a deep drag. A long moment passes. Then:

Amar EXHALES the cigarette smoke!

> RUHI
> Goodbye, Amar.

REVEAL: RUHI IS ALONE. THERE IS NO AMAR.

> RUHI
> The lie is our truth.

Ruhi picks up the photo frame and looks at the photo.

RUHI'S POV: IN THE PHOTO - Ruhi and an INDIAN WOMAN.

Ruhi -- her expression soft and vulnerable, runs her fingers over the Indian Woman's smiling face.

> RUHI
> I miss you. I will always miss you,
> my love.

Ruhi -- all alone in the apartment. As she stares out at the city view.

WE HEAR a distant scream.

**EXT. NYC SKYLINE - NIGHT**

WE HEAR a ferry, a woman drowning underwater. Then, Silence.

> FADE OUT.

**THE END**

# HOLDEN

**INT. NEW YORK CITY APARTMENT - DAY**

CLOSE ON: JANE, late 20s. She's holding gaze intently with--

CLOSE ON: HOLDEN, late 20s, uncomfortable, a LONG KNIFE in his hand.

Jane and Holden are sitting at a dining table facing each other. You can cut the tension between them with a knife.

> HOLDEN
> You know I love you.

Jane thrusts a PHOTOGRAPH she's holding towards him. WE DON'T SEE WHAT'S IN IT. Holden doesn't even glance at it.

> JANE
> Do you love her too?

> HOLDEN
> She's not in my life. You are.

> JANE
> Why didn't you tell me about her?

> HOLDEN
> She's not relevant to our relationship.

Jane holds a PHOTOGRAPH up to Holden who looks at it. WE DON'T SEE WHO'S IN THE PHOTO.

> JANE
> You are married to her. That's relevant.

> HOLDEN
> No, I'm not.

> JANE
> County records say you are.

> HOLDEN
> She's married to Angel. Not me.

> JANE
> That used to be your name. Angel.

                    HOLDEN
          Not anymore. I am Holden, now. And
          I'm not married.

Holden pushes her hand with the photograph down. Jane places
the photo facedown on the table.

                    JANE
          That's not how this works.

                    HOLDEN
          It has to work this way.

                    JANE
          You lied to me, Angel or Holden or
          whatever you want to call yourself.

                    HOLDEN
          You went behind my back. Digging
          into my past...

                    JANE
          Only because I was worried, my
          love.

                    HOLDEN
          About what? Angel is gone. So is
          Priyanka.

                    JANE
          She's still your wife...

                    HOLDEN
          She's Angel's wife. Let it go.

                    JANE
          I will when you divorce her.

                    HOLDEN
          She ghosted me. I can't divorce her
          when I can't find her. I've tried,
          believe me, but she's gone. That's
          why I had to get a new identity, a
          fresh start. When I met you... that
          was the happiest moment of my life.

                    JANE
          Mine too.

They smile at each other.

                    JANE
          But you have to tell me the truth.

                    HOLDEN
          This is the truth.
          (sees knife in his hand)
          Can I go make dinner now? I got an
          exquisite bottle of Port wine you
          are gonna love.

                    JANE
          Okay.

JANE's eyes hold a mix of vulnerability and strength. She
watches Holden through the serving hatch. Holden smiles at
her as he prepares dinner.


**INT. BATHROOM - DAY**

Jane enters.

She looks down at the BLUE ENGAGEMENT RING BOX in the palm
of her hand.

Looks back up at her REFLECTION in the BATHROOM MIRROR,
split across two panels of the mirror.


**INT. KITCHEN - DAY**

CLOSE ON: CUTTING BOARD. A KNIFE viciously cuts a RED TOMATO
into two.

HOLDEN, late 20s, wipes his brow as he continues to chop.

CLOSE ON: CUTTING BOARD. The KNIFE CUTS THROUGH AN ONION
revealing the layers inside.

The chopped tomato sits like a bloody pile in one corner of
the board.

CLOSE ON: A PAN, sizzling oil. The cut onions are thrown in.

Holden, intent on the task at hand.

MUSIC begins to play. A dancey tune.

Filled with anticipation, he smiles as he wipes his hands on
the apron and steps out of the kitchen.


**INT. DINING AREA - DAY**

Holden leans on the wall and watches with a smile.

Jane -- dances and sways to the music. Enticing. The way an

escort would for a valued client.

>                    HOLDEN
>          How I missed you... Life is dark
>          without you, Jane.

Jane walks up to him, and puts a finger to her lips.

>                    JANE
>          Shhh...

They stand there. In love.

>                    HOLDEN
>          Hungry?

Jane nods. A smile on her face, fondness in her eyes.

## INT. DINING AREA - NIGHT

Holden watches with a smile as Jane finishes her last bite.
He pours Port wine in two glasses and hands one to her.

>                    HOLDEN
>          Tchin Tchin.

Holden takes a sip. Jane doesn't. Places her glass on the
table and watches him with a curious expression.

>                    HOLDEN
>          What?

>                    JANE
>          I have questions.

>                    HOLDEN
>          Jane, we are past this.

She PLACES the engagement ring box on the table and pushes
it gently and slowly across the table towards him.

Holden's grin dies when he sees the box.

>                    HOLDEN
>          You went through my things?

>                    JANE
>          There's a wedding band in there,
>          Holden, and it's not my size. You
>          kept your wife's rings?

>                    HOLDEN
>          So what? It's always drama with

                    you. Stop this shit.

Holden gets up and steps away from her. Jane rushes him and
pushes him into the wall.

                    JANE
          I wanted to be your betrothed.

                    HOLDEN
          Jane, calm down.

                    JANE
          ...and then I find out the truth.
          The love of my life is a lying
          cheat... a married man. That's
          shit. That's drama.

Jane pushes him hard again. Holden gathers himself and walks
into the kitchen.

Holden, sour expression on his face, starts cleaning a dish.

Jane crosses over to face him through the serving hatch.

Holden HOLDS the KNIFE under running water to clean it.

Jane's gaze travels to the knife still in Holden's hand.

                    JANE
          Put the knife down.

                    HOLDEN
          (scoffs)
          What? Why?

                    JANE
          Don't think you can do to me what
          you did to your wife.

                    HOLDEN
          I'm not gonna hurt you, Jane.

                    JANE
          Put the knife down, or I'll scream
          for help so loud...

                    HOLDEN
          Stop your paranoid shit.

                    JANE
          Three... Two... One...

Holden drops the knife into the sink. Steps back. Rubs his
face. Can't believe this shit is happening.

                    HOLDEN
          Next time, take your goddamn meds
          before you come knocking.

Jane turns and walks away.

NEAR THE SOFA

Jane slumps down on the sofa. Holden is still near the sink.
They both stare forward.

                    HOLDEN
          Are we ever gonna get over this?

                    JANE
          Only if you tell me the truth.

                    HOLDEN
          Okay. I want this behind us.

                    JANE
          When was the last time you saw your
          wife?

                    HOLDEN
          January of last year. I took her to
          Portugal for one last shot at
          saving our marriage.

INSERT PHOTO: Belém Tower, Portugal

                    HOLDEN
          On the last day of our stay, she
          insisted on going to the beach in
          Troia where we had first met. I
          thought she was softening towards
          me, but she was just exorcizing the
          last good memory she had of us
          together.

INSERT PHOTO: Peninsula De Troia, Portugal

                    HOLDEN
          On the ferry ride back, she stood
          on the deck, all alone, smiling
          into the freezing wind.
              (long exhale)
          I went up to her and she told me.
          It's over, she said. I'm going back
          to India, she said. You are a free
          man, she said. Then was gone. I
          stood there, frozen in tears...
          Never saw her again.

INSERT VIDEO: A WAVE CRASHES ONTO A BEACH

> HOLDEN
> That's the truth.

> JANE
> Oh Holden. I needed to hear that.

> HOLDEN
> I should have told you. I'm sorry.

Jane and Holden come together. They kiss.

Then -- Jane pulls back and speaks in an almost-whisper.

> JANE
> Priyanka's body washed ashore on a
> Troia beach three weeks after you
> returned to the States. I don't
> think she went back to India. She
> must have returned to Troia. But I
> know you didn't have anything to do
> with it.

Holden blinks.

> HOLDEN
> She's not dead. She can't be dead.

> JANE
> There's a warrant out for Angel's
> arrest. You are a suspect, Holden.

> HOLDEN
> I didn't hurt her. I'd never have
> hurt her. They are wrong.

> JANE
> Doesn't matter, my love. Doesn't
> matter what the world believes. All
> that matters is what you and I
> believe. And I believe you. We know
> the truth, you and I.

Jane sits down at the dining table and lights a CIGARETTE.
She exhales in relief.

> JANE
> I'll never leave you now.

Holden stares at her for a moment. Lost in his thoughts
Then, he walks over and sits facing her.

He sees the ENGAGEMENT RING BOX on the table. He reaches out

and picks it up. He picks up a PHOTOGRAPH under the box. He
looks at it. WE DO NOT SEE what's in the photo.

> HOLDEN
> Angel.

> JANE
> (exhales smoke)
> What?

> HOLDEN
> Truth is freedom. It's freezing.

> JANE
> Come, my love. I'll warm you up.

Holden stands up and walks away from the table and stands
with his back to her.

> HOLDEN
> On the ferry ride back, she stood
> on the deck, all alone...

> JANE
> Holden...

Jane stands up, concerned. She walks to him and grabs him by
the shoulder and turns him to face her.

> HOLDEN
> ...smiling into the freezing wind.

> JANE
> Don't. Stop.

> HOLDEN
> Staring out at the sunset over the
> Arrabida mountains.

Jane screams into his face. Holden grabs her by the
shoulder. They are locked in a strong braced position.

> JANE
> I said stop.

> HOLDEN
> Fado's music played in the
> background. I stood next to her.
> Hoping she'd accept me. But she
> pushed me away with so much
> contempt. I felt it. I  felt...

> JANE
> ...her complete rejection.

                    HOLDEN
          I tried to hold her hand. She
          slapped me.

Jane slaps him.

                    HOLDEN
          I got angry. And I...

                    JANE
          ...pushed her...

Jane pushes Holden. He hits the wall, but is unconcerned.

                    HOLDEN
          She went over the railing. I saw
          her...

                    JANE
          ...hit the water.

They fall to the ground.

                    HOLDEN
          Her eyes, filled with such hate for
          me. I wanted to...

                    JANE
          ...jump into the water...

                    HOLDEN
          ...to save her, but I didn't.

Jane and Holden - both on the floor, defeated.

                    JANE
          Oh Holden... Why did you do this?

                    HOLDEN
          You wanted the truth.

                    JANE
          I needed you to lie, to convince me
          it was the truth. You gave me a
          goddamn confession.

                    JANE
          You don't know anything. You hear
          me? Nothing.

Jane, furious, tries to gather herself.

>           HOLDEN
> It's getting dark... No. Help me.

>           JANE
> Shhh...

>           HOLDEN
> Please don't make it dark.

>           JANE
> You are just... no use to me if you
> cannot lie.

Jane takes a deep drag, a cold air around her.

JANE'S POV: Holden EXHALES the cigarette smoke!

>           HOLDEN
> I know who you are. I know what you
> did, Angel.

Holden holds up the PHOTOGRAPH in front of Jane. WE DON'T
SEE WHO'S IN IT. Jane TAKES the photograph.
CUT TO:


**REVEAL - JANE ALONE AT THE TABLE. THERE IS NO HOLDEN.**

Jane is HOLDING THE PHOTOGRAPH and is looking at it.

ANGLE ON PHOTO: JANE with ANOTHER WOMAN, presumably
PRIYANKA.

Clearly lovers.

In happier times.

>           JANE
> Truth is death, Holden.


**THE END**

# YOUR ONLY HOPE

**INT. STATION WAGON - DUSK**

A MAN, known simply as HOLDEN, late 20s, stares balefully forward as the car moves through the outskirts of suburbia.

                    WOMAN (O.S.)
          Holden?

Holden doesn't respond.

                    WOMAN (O.S.)
          Holden!

Holden turns towards the passenger side. The woman is in her late 20s. She watches him curiously for a moment, then holds up a pack of cigarettes.

                    WOMAN
          Its your last one!

                    HOLDEN
          You can have it.

                    WOMAN
          Thanks. These kill, you know.

Holden seems irritated at that remark.

The woman lights up using a cigarette lighter. A deep breath. She sighs out the smoke.

                    WOMAN
          Stop being so lost in your head.
          Talk to me.

                    HOLDEN
          What for?

                    WOMAN
          Make this a pleasant goodbye.

                    HOLDEN
          Fuck pleasant goodbye. I hate
          fucking pleasant fucking good
          fucking byes.

                    WOMAN
          Suit yourself.

Silence in the car as the woman continues to smoke and look outside at the rolling imagery of American suburbia. A strip mall. Row of houses. A gas station.

The car pulls into a gas station.

                    WOMAN
          You don't need gas.

                    HOLDEN
          I needs smokes.

He leaves.

The Woman makes a decision and quickly opens her purse and pulls out a pistol. She pops the magazine out. Checks to see if its loaded.

It is.

She snaps the magazine back into the pistol. She picks up his cellphone and looks at it.

Through the driver's side window, we see Holden walking back towards the car.

She hides the pistol on her side as opens the door and gets in the car.

He starts the car, and lights up.

The car screeches out of the gas station.

The car travels on a country road.

                    HOLDEN
          Where do you want me to drop you?

                    WOMAN
          What if I said I love you?
              (off no response)
          What if I said I like you?
              (off no response)
          Drop me off near the beach.

Holden looks at her for a moment then looks back at the road.

                    HOLDEN
          We should be together.

The woman laughs heartily. Holden ignores her as he continues...

                    HOLDEN
Mucho together. For mucho, mucho
time.

                    WOMAN
Holden, NO!

                    HOLDEN
Marry me.

                    WOMAN
NO!

Holden pulls the car over.

                    HOLDEN
Get the fuck out of my car.

                    WOMAN
Your wife's car.

Holden is taken aback.

                    HOLDEN
What?

                    WOMAN
Your fucking wife's car. This is
your wife's fucking car.

                    HOLDEN
How did you know?

                    WOMAN
Not from you. I know you didn't
tell, you married bastard.

                    HOLDEN
I was a long time ago.

                    WOMAN
You are not divorced. I know.

                    HOLDEN
Fuck! Fuck! You been snooping on
me?

                    WOMAN
         (firm)
Where is she, Holden?

                    HOLDEN
Wh... she... she left me. She went
away. Maybe back to India. That's

where she was from. I don't know.

> WOMAN
> Liar.

Holden turns and stares at the cold pistol pointed at him.

The woman has become serious - there is a perceptibly yet subtle mood shift.

> WOMAN
> How did it end?

> HOLDEN
> I... I don't remember.

> WOMAN
> How did it end, Holden?

> HOLDEN
> Funny thing is... I don't remember.
> The last thing I remember, I...
>> (beat)
> I... we had gone to Lisbon,
> Portugal. It was a make-or-break
> vacation for our relationship.
> We... had walked around in Rossio,
> she bought a few things, then we
> drove down to a small town Setubal.
> And then... the next thing I
> remember is the immigration
> official at Newark, welcoming me
> back. And I said to him, obrigado
> mother fucker.

Holden starts laughing.

> HOLDEN
> You should have seen his face.
> Obrigado motherfucker. Obrigado!
> That's portugese for 'thank you'.

> WOMAN
> How did it end?

> HOLDEN
> I told you. She probably went back
> to India. That's where she was
> from.

> WOMAN
>> (shakes her head 'no')
> I checked with her family.

                    HOLDEN
          What the fuck? You called her
          family?

The woman turns on him fiercely. Startles him.

                    WOMAN
          Did you kill her, Holden?

Holden rises angrily, and fist bunched, he is ready to
strike her despite the pistol pointed at him. But the woman
doesn't flinch.

                    HOLDEN
          You a cop?

                    WOMAN
          No.

                    HOLDEN
          Did my wife's family hire you?

                    WOMAN
          No.

                    HOLDEN
          Who the fuck are you?

                    WOMAN
          I am your only hope.

Holden regains control, and he settles back down.

                    WOMAN
          Why did you kill her, Holden?

                    HOLDEN
          It doesn't matter.

                    WOMAN
          Answer my question Holden.

                    HOLDEN
             (swirls on her)
          I don't have to fuckin' answer
          anything. Get the fuck out. Get
          out. Now!
             (slams the wheel)
          AH!

He gets out of the car and slams the door shut. We see him
from inside the car. He furiously paces outside the window.

                    HOLDEN
              (screaming to himself)
     I told Mr. Jones. I told that
     fucking bastard, he should just
     kill me. He should just kill me.
     Just fuckin' kill me. But he
     didn't... and I had to kill her.
              (sobs)
     And my sweet little...my sweet...

The woman gets out of the car and goes to him and comforts
him as we watch both from inside the car.


**INT. CAR - NIGHT - ON THE BEACH - LATER**

Holden and the woman are in the car. Holden looks resigned.
And very calm.

                    HOLDEN
     We were at a the cathedral in
     Lisbon. She lit a candle there. I
     was watching her. She looked sad.
     Lost. Distant. I didn't even need
     her to tell me. But she did. She
     told me it was over. She had been
     feeling the distance grow between
     us ever since our daughter
     disappeared. She had already bought
     her ticket to India. I convinced
     her to give me one last chance to
     try and talk her out of it. I told
     her I deserved that one day. For
     all the time we had spent together.
     She agreed. I chartered a boat and
     we went out together. Deep sea
     fishing I told her.
              (beat)
     I came back alone. The next day I
     flew back to Newark. Meet with Mr.
     Jones. Give him the status update.
     I did what I had to.


                    WOMAN
     You could have said no to Mr.
     Jones.

Holden laughs - the meaning is clear.

                    WOMAN
     You fucking murderer.

Holden reaches for the pistol. She resists but does not
shoot. He manages to pull the pistol out of her hand. He

aims the pistol at her temple.

> WOMAN
> You want to kill me? You fucking
> bastard.

> HOLDEN
> You can't live now. Mr. Jones
> wouldn't like it.

> WOMAN
> You've gone crazy Holden. Who is
> this, Mr. Jones? Fuck Mr. Jones.
> Fuck what he says.

> HOLDEN
> You don't know anything. You don't
> know what's happening around you.
> In this world. You don't know
> what's happening to human beings.
> To human societies. Mr. Jones...
> he... he knows. He knows what to
> do. To fix it. I believe in him.

> WOMAN
> I don't.

COP CARS and SIRENS are heard in the distance increasing in
volume.

> WOMAN
> (holding up her cell
> phone)
> I called them Holden. They'll get
> you, and they'll get this Mr.
> Jones.

> HOLDEN
> You must die.

> WOMAN
> Because Mr. Jones says so?

> HOLDEN
> I love you.

> WOMAN
> Like you loved your wife?

> HOLDEN
> She didn't have faith. She refused
> to believe?

> WOMAN
>
> Faith? Belief? So you can kill the
> ones you love? She didn't want to
> kill her daughter for her faith,
> you sick, sick man.

> HOLDEN
>
> I can't say no to Mr. Jones.

> WOMAN
>
> Then kill yourself asshole.

Holden licks his now dry, nervous lips. And then begins to
squeeze the trigger. He is incredibly calm. The woman is
sobbing hysterically.

> WOMAN (O.S.)
>
> Go ahead, do it, just do it. There
> won't be anymore pain.

We continue to watch Holden as he struggles.

The SIRENS grow in intensity.

We cut to the woman, but there is NO ONE there. Holden is
pointing the gun at empty space.

We still hear the WOMAN speak. But the voice has an
ethereal, disconnected quality to it.

> WOMAN (O.S.)
>
> End it, Holden. Don't let Mr. Jones
> into your soul.

We see Holden's hand move back towards him. We continue to
look at the empty passenger seat.

> WOMAN (O.S.)
> (screaming)
> Do it, just do it. There won't be
> anymore pain. Kill me Holden. Kill
> me like you killed your daughter
> and your wife. For Mr. Jones. For
> Mr. Jones!

We hear a SHOT. As the echo of the shot fades away, all is
quiet except for the chirping of the birds.

**THE END**

# Chapter Three

## About "Le Nid" & "Leaving Priyanka"

Espionage thrillers have always been a passion of mine.

As a teenager, I devoured Robert Ludlum—The Bourne Identity and beyond—which sparked a lifelong love of spy stories. I'm also a Francophile and have made many efforts over the years to learn French. These twin loves power the two scripts in this chapter.

LE NID is a French–English thriller originally envisioned for Paris. Ultimately, I ended up rewriting it for French-speaking actors in New York City. A more realistic goal given the finances available (none really!).

This New York metro area based version—where I live and have practical access to resources—remains unproduced for now. It's part of a larger spy universe I'm determined to bring to the screen someday.

LEAVING PRIYANKA let me explore India's external intelligence agency, RAW (Research and Analysis Wing), as a testing ground for future projects. I have a TV series and a feature in development in this world, and this short served as an exploration of tone and genre. We shot near the iconic United Nations Headquarters in New York City.

Both scripts are tailored for low- to no-budget execution. I design my shorts to be producible on very little, and I'll compromise where needed—even on some story elements—to achieve that goal. The aim isn't to make "calling cards"; it's to explore genre, tone, character, and location.

These shorts are made for one reason alone: to learn.

I hope you enjoy these scripts.

# THE NEST (*Le Nid*)

**EXT. NEW YORK CAFE - DAY**

SUMMER DAY. Bustling. A YOUNG WOMAN, 30s, smiling, happy, perhaps in love, makes her way through the crowd.

She steps into a CAFE.

MOMENTS LATER - THREE MEN, dressed similarly in a mix of muted SUITS and JACKETS converge at the entrance.

They look at each other. One takes out a PHONE and listens for a moment. He hangs up. Nods a 'yes' to the other two.

They enter.

**INT. CAFE - DAY**

The young woman takes a seat and is about to sip her COFFEE when the three men surround her.

Her smile fades.

**INT. INTERROGATION ROOM - INDETERMINATE TIME**

HUNCHED FORM on a CHAIR in the distance.

TOO FAR to tell if its a man or a woman. Leaning forward, held only by the hands presumably tied behind the back of the chair.

HARSH light almost drowns out the form in brightness. The rest of the room drowned in POOLS of darkness and shadows.

CLANG OF A METALLIC DOOR shutting. FOOTSTEPS on the floor.

A POLISHED LEATHER SHOE blocks out the form in the distance, then moves towards the chair.

The MAN has his back to us, and is dressed in a SUIT. He pauses to light TWO CIGARETTES held casually between his lips.

The LIGHT reveals a handsome, warm face, cold eyes, probably in his 30s. He watches the form on the chair for a moment. Still holding both cigarettes, now lit, between his lips --

                    MAN
          Tu veux une cigarette?
          You want a cigarette?

The person on the chair tenses, then looks up. Its the WOMAN
FROM THE CAFE, her beautiful face now bruised.

Confusion on her face makes way for anger.

                    WOMAN
          Toi! Un flic? Salaud!
          You! A Cop! Bastard!

                    MAN
          Calme toi!
          Calm down!

With a grin, he walks upto her and puts a CIGARETTE in her
mouth even as his own dangles from his lips.

                    MAN
          Je sais! Tu detestes les flics! Je
          comprends! Nom de dieu!
          I know. You hate cops. I get it.
          Damn!

                    WOMAN
          Alors. Tout cela c'était un
          mensonge?
          So it was all a lie?

                    MAN
          Bien fait, Sherlock! Tu veux une
          clope ou pas?
          Well done, Sherlock. Do you wish to
          smoke, or no?

She takes a drag.

                    WOMAN
          C'était pas un mensonge. Je l'ai
          senti. C'était vrai.
          It was not all a lie. I felt it. It
          was real.

                    MAN
          Ils m'ont accordé dix minutes pour
          parler avec toi, toute seule. Je
          leur ai promis de sortir d'ici avec
          un nom et une adresse. Cette fois-
          ci, avec un vrai nom et une vraie
          adresse. Et je te jure, tu mourras
          sans souffrir.
          They gave me ten minutes with you

alone. I told them I would walk out
of here with a name and a location,
this time, a real name and a real
location, and I promise, you will
die without pain.

                    WOMAN
          Va te faire foutre! Tu sais bien
          que c'est pas moi. Je ne suis pas
          ce qu'ils pensent!
          Go jump in a pile of shit! You know
          I'm not what they think I am.

                    MAN
          Un vrai nom. Une vraie adresse. Une
          mort sans souffrance.
          A real name and location. A
          painless death. Its a "good deal"
          as your people say.

The woman spits in his direction. The man's SHADOW on the
wall moves - and we see his hand slap her.

                    WOMAN
          Détache-moi, si t'es un homme,
          essaie encore!
          If you are a man, uncuff me and try
          that again.

The man grins, then, UNCUFFS her hands and steps back.

Surprised, she rubs her wrists. He watches quietly,
finishing the last drag on his cigarette. He lets it fall to
the ground and squashes it with his shoe.

                    MAN
          Je peux pas le croire. Tu demeures
          si belle.
          I can't believe you still look so
          beautiful.

                    WOMAN
          Va te faire foutre.
          Go to hell.

                    MAN
          Qu'est-ce que faisais sur la place?
          What were you doing in the square?

                    WOMAN
          Je visitais le Musee...
          L'exposition de Van Gogh... tu sais
          bien.
          I was going to the museum... to the

Van Gogh exhibit... you know that.

                    MAN
          Nous étions censés de se retrouver
          après pour un café. Oui, je sais
          bien. Dis-moi ce que je sais pas.
          We were supposed to meet after for
          coffee. Yes, I know that. Tell me
          what I don't know.

The Man regards her for a long time -- then he gently
caresses her chin.

                    MAN
          L'Ope était deja en route, oui ou
          non?
          The operation was already in
          motion, was it not?

The woman's voice is bitter --

                    WOMAN
          Tu sais que je ne pouvais apeine
          attendre d'etre dans tes bras?
          Salaud! Tu sais ca?
          All I know is that I could barely
          wait until I held you in my arms
          again! You bastard! Did you know
          that?

She spits in his face.

                    MAN
          Pour les trois mois que nous avons
          vécu ensemble...
          For those three months we lived
          together...

Interrupting him --

                    WOMAN
          Les plus beaux trois mois de ma
          vie...
          The most beautiful, beautiful three
          months of my life...

Ignoring her --

                    MAN
          Je t'ai administré un médicament
          tous les jours. Il agit lentement.
          Les dosages sont faibles, ils sont
          indétectables par les tests. Cela
          t'a fait parler dans ton sommeil.

> Je t'ai entendu dire des choses...
> I administered a drug to you
> everyday. It acts slowly. The
> dosages are small, so they are
> undetectable by your tests. It
> makes you talk in your sleep. I
> heard you say things...

He pauses significantly -- the woman scoffs in disbelief!

> WOMAN
> Rêves! Tu parle de rêves! Je ne
> suis pas responsable de mes pensées
> quand je dors! Je lis les
> journaux... Je sais ce qui se
> passe... Je suis affecté par tout
> ca! Je pense à ces choses! J'ai
> peur! Comme tout le monde. Ca ne
> veut pas dire que j'en suis un!
> Dreams! You talk of dreams! I'm not
> responsible for my thoughts when I
> sleep! I read the newspapers... I
> know what's going on... I am
> affected by it! I think about it! I
> have fears! Like everyone else.
> That doesn't make me one of THEM!

The man takes out a SET OF PHOTOS and spreads them out in
front of her. SHOTS of the WOMAN wearing CAMOUFLAGE, HOLDING
VARIOUS GUNS.

The woman is shocked into silence.

> MAN
> Il rest sept minutes.
> You have seven minutes left.

The woman switches to English. So does the man.

> WOMAN
> Two years ago, there was a man.
> He...

> MAN
> Forced you? Huh? Stop lying!

> WOMAN
> I was in love. I thought I was in
> love.

> MAN
> Love, huh? You fall in love rather
> easily, don't you?

                    WOMAN
          I thought I was going to have a
          life with him. He told me that his
          cause was just... that his people
          were good. I didn't believe him.
          But he wanted... he said he wanted
          to see me as a warrior. That's when
          he dressed me up, and took these
          photos.

                    MAN
          You don't happen to have his name
          and location, would you?

The woman shakes her head 'no', and the man laughs - his
laughter stained with sarcasm.

The woman tries to convince him.

                    WOMAN
          A month after these photos were
          taken, he disappeared! The
          apartment he took me to, wasn't
          even his! The people who lived
          there had gone on vacation and he
          must have broken in! I guess. I
          don't know. I don't know anything!

She pauses.

                    WOMAN
          You knew about these photos when
          you met me...

                    MAN
          I met you because of these photos.

                    WOMAN
          You were watching me?

                    MAN
          Ofcourse. For two years.

                    WOMAN
          Then, you know, I have had nothing
          to do with this man...

He pauses.

                    MAN
          I know. They don't.

The woman gets up and goes to him. They switch languages
now-- playing a game of cat and mouse.

                    WOMAN
          Sauve-moi!
          Save me!

               MAN
          Je peux pas.
          I can't.

                    WOMAN
          Alors! Au moins, crois moi.
          Regarde! Tu peux pas voir que je
          dis la vérité?
          Then at least believe me! Look into
          my eyes. Look! Can't you see I'm
          telling you the truth?

               MAN
          Même si c'est vrai, ca change rien.
          T'es déjà morte.
          Even if you are, its no use. You
          are dead already.

                    WOMAN
          Tue moi, alors, si c'est ma seule
          isso.
          Kill me then. Let that be my
          escape.

                    MAN
          Okay.

He draws his GLOCK 9MM and points it at her. She closes her
eyes.

                    WOMAN
          Mon seul regret, c'est que tu ne me
          crois pas.
          My only regret is that you don't
          believe me.

She waits. Nothing. She opens her eyes. The man has lowered
his gun.

                    WOMAN
          Tu me crois.
          You believe me.

The man nods, slowly, sadly, after a long time.

They kiss.

                    WOMAN
          Dites leur, alors. Ils te croirant!
          Then tell them. They'll believe

you!

                    MAN
          Ca me rendra suspect.
          I'll only fall under suspicion.

                    WOMAN
          Tu sais qu'ils vont me faire. Ils
          pensent que j'ai des informations!
          Je ne sais rien, moi! Mais ils me
          croiront pas! Il faut que tu me
          tue! Tue moi!
          You know what they'll do to me...
          They think I have information! I
          don't know anything, but they don't
          believe me! They'll... they'll...
          kill me!

                    MAN
          Prends-moi en otage! Tu peux t'en
          sortir. Il ya une voiture qui
          attend sur la Rue de Lyon.
          Take me hostage! You can get out.
          There's a car waiting on Rue de
          Lyon.

                    WOMAN
          Est-ce que ca va marcher?
          Will it work?

                    MAN
          Je t'aime.
          I love you.

They kiss. Urgently. The man pleads.

                    MAN
          Ecoute-moi! Prends-moi en otage!

He takes out the MAGAZINE of the GLOCK 9MM -

                    MAN
          Nine rounds! And I have an extra
          magazine. We'll shoot our way out
          of here.

He puts the magazine back into the GLOCK and hands it to
her. She takes it hesitantly.

                    WOMAN
          I've never shot a gun before.

                    MAN
          Its easy. Just point. And pull the

>                    trigger. Don't worry, they won't
>                    shoot you - if they wanted you
>                    dead, they'd have killed you a long
>                    time ago.

>                         WOMAN
>                    Okay.
>                         (beat)
>                    Donne moi ton revolver. Je vais le
>                    faire.
>                    Okay. Give me your gun! I'll do it.

She grabs his gun. He lets her take it. There's a moment of
tension as its unclear what she'll use the gun for. She puts
it to her temple -

>                         WOMAN
>                    Non. Ca te rendra suspect. Je
>                    t'aime.
>                    You'll only fall under suspicion. I
>                    love you.

>                         MAN
>                    Arrete!

She PULLS the trigger.

CLICK.

The hammer falls impotently on an empty chamber.

The woman opens her eyes -- confused. A MALE VOICE booms out
on an unseen loudspeaker.

>                         MALE VOICE (O.S.)
>                    D'accord. Elle est claire.
>                    Ok. She's clear.

>                         MAN
>                    Oui, monsieur.
>                    Yes sir.

>                         MALE VOICE (O.S.)
>                    Lâche-la.
>                    Let her go.

>                         MAN
>                    Vous avez passé le test.
>                    You passed the test.

>                         WOMAN
>                    Le test?

>                    MAN
>          On vous surveillait pour voir si
>          vous mentiez. C'était la seule
>          façon d'être sûr.
>          You were being monitored to see if
>          you were lying. This was the only
>          way we could be sure.

The woman -- stunned silence. The man walks up and takes his revolver back.

He pulls back the hammer and shows her --

>                    MAN
>          No firing pin. This gun could never
>          fire a bullet.

>                    WOMAN
>          Alors. Tout cela c'était un
>          mensonge.
>          So, it was all a lie.

>                    MAN
>          Vous pouvez y aller, mademoiselle.
>          You can go.

The woman, speechless, walks towards the door.

>                    MAN
>          Attendez!
>          Wait!

The woman stops but does not turn back.

>                    MAN
>          Je vous ai jamais aimé. Je faisais
>          mon boulot, c'est tout.
>          I never loved you. I was only doing
>          my job.

The woman glares at him for a moment - her feelings indecipherable. She leaves.

The man keeps looking where she was standing, lost in thought when the booming voice on the loudspeaker interrupts him --

>                    MALE VOICE (O.S.)
>          Tu pense qu'elle l'y a cru?
>          You think she fell for it?

The man doesn't reply. He lights ANOTHER CIGARETTE. He smiles, but his cold eyes don't.

>                    MAN
>           C'est une sacree menteuse, mais je
>           suis meilleure qu'elle. Mettez
>           notre meilleur agent a so trouces.
>           Elle va nous conduire directment au
>           nid de...
>           She's a good liar, but I'm better.
>           Put your best agent on her tail.
>           She'll lead us to the nest of...

He never finishes that sentence - pouring his energy into
crushing the cigarette under the sole of his SHINING SHOE.


**EXT. CITY - DAY**

The woman walks in the sunlight - and the CROWD. Her eyes
meet with a MAN standing in the doorway reading a NEWSPAPER.
He seems to be watching her, then quickly averts his gaze.


**INT. SUBWAY - DAY**

In the subway car. ANOTHER MAN seems to be watching her.


**EXT. STREET - DAY**

The woman emerges from the subway station.

>                  WOMAN (V.O.)
>           I knew the gun wouldn't fire. The
>           firing pin was gone. Oldest trick
>           in the book. The cops really are
>           incompetent. Now they must believe
>           I'm part of the Nest. Anyone else
>           would have tried to escape, not
>           kill themselves. He'll have his
>           best agents on my tail. Everything
>           went as I had planned. Now I'm a
>           marked woman. And its only a matter
>           of time before the Nest finds me,
>           and tries to recruit me. All I can
>           do now is wait. And be ready.


**<u>FIN</u>**

# LEAVING PRIYANKA

**EXT. NEW YORK - NEAR THE UNITED NATIONS - DAY**

The city of New York. Traffic. Buildings. Waterfront.

And the UNITED NATIONS BUILDING.

**EXT. STREET - NEAR THE UN - DAY**

ABHAY (30), dressed in business casual, crosses the street.

**EXT. BENCH - TUDOR CITY - DAY**

Abhay sits on a bench. Dials a number. He seems nervous, but puts on a confident face.

>                     ABHAY
> Hey. It's me, Abhay. We met a
> couple of nights ago... you were
> with your friends, I was with my
> friends, and we ditched them...
> yeah. Yes, that's me. Glad you
> remember me.
>           (listens)
> Of course, I remember your name.
> Priyanka.
>           (listens, looks at his
>            watch)
> Today? Yeah, sure, I can make it
> there by five. I won't be late.

**INT. PRIYANKA'S LIVING ROOM - DAY**

A WOMAN says bye to DEPARTING GUESTS off screen as we watch Abhay looking at a painting.

>                  WOMAN (O.S.)
> Thanks for coming. See you.

The Woman walks up to Abhay.

PRIYANKA (26), the woman, walks up to Abhay.

>                     ABHAY
> I'm really sorry I was late.

                    PRIYANKA
          What held you up?

                    ABHAY
                (nervous laugh)
          I just got caught up at work...

                    PRIYANKA
          Ah. Work. Let's not talk about
          work, and I'll forgive you for
          being late by twenty seven minutes.
          Deal?

                    ABHAY
          Deal.

Abhay exhales, as relief floods over him.

                    ABHAY
          So when did you paint this?

                    PRIYANKA
          Recently.

                    ABHAY
          It's funny, but this reminds me of
          when I was ten years old. I had
          gone to Paris and I met this girl.
          It was the first time I said, "I
          love you". I had no idea what it
          all meant, you know.

                    PRIYANKA
          Your first love.

                    ABHAY
          Could have been my last.

Abhay leans in to kiss her on the lips. She stops him with
her palm on his chest. She gestures 'a little' with her
thumb and index finger.

                    PRIYANKA
          Little too fast.

                    ABHAY
          I like fast.

Beat.

Priyanka leans in. They kiss.

                                        CUT TO:

**EXT. NYC STREETS - DAY**

Street signs of TUDOR CITY. As day turns to night --

**INT. PRIYANKA'S BEDROOM - DUSK**

They lie in bed. Post-coital. Priyanka turns to Abhay and smiles. Abhay smiles back.

> ABHAY
> Pri... Can I call you that?

> PRIYANKA
> You just did, man. Too late to ask
> for permission.

They both laugh. A beat of silence.

> PRIYANKA
> You know, my father used to call my
> mother that.

> ABHAY
> She had the same name as you?

> PRIYANKA
> She came before me, silly. I have
> the same name as her.
> (gentle sigh)
> After my mom died, no one said that
> name again. Until now.

> ABHAY
> I'm sorry about your mom.

> PRIYANKA
> It's okay. It was a long time ago.
> (beat)
> She'd have liked you.

> ABHAY
> Not if she knew we'd do this.

> PRIYANKA
> (laughs)
> And on our first date!

> ABHAY
> (laughs)
> Wait, so this is a date!

> PRIYANKA
> This? I don't know what this is.

Abhay leans in -- they kiss.

>                    PRIYANKA
>           Or that. I don't know what that is
>           either.

>                    ABHAY
>           Just a casual kiss.

## INT. BEDROOM - DAY

Priyanka and Abhay eat out of a tub of ice-cream in bed.

>                    PRIYANKA
>           Okay. This is a date.
>                (off his grin)
>           And no, you are not staying over
>           tonight.

>                    ABHAY
>           I didn't ask...

>                    PRIYANKA
>           I could see it in your eyes. The
>           desperation.

>                    ABHAY
>           Oh. Harsh.
>                (beat)
>           You know, I make a really nice
>           breakfast...

>                    PRIYANKA
>           Ooh. Sounds nice. But no. You are
>           not staying over.
>                (beat)
>           Don't you have to go to work
>           tomorrow?

>                    ABHAY
>           The UN is closed for Eid.
>                (off her look)
>           It's a muslim festival...

>                    PRIYANKA
>           I know what Eid is.
>                (beat)
>           You work for the UN? When we met at
>           the party yesterday, I thought you
>           were a doctor.

>                    ABHAY
>           What? Why?

                    PRIYANKA
          You had such a scientific
          explanation for your perfect
          hangover remedy while I puked my
          guts out...

                    ABHAY
          Did my remedy work?

                    PRIYANKA
          It did. And now, it's time for you
          to go home. I have things to do.

                    ABHAY
          How about lunch tomorrow near your
          office?

                    PRIYANKA
          Can't. We're closed for Eid too.

                    ABHAY
          Really? Where do you work?

                    PRIYANKA
          I'm a consular officer at the
          Pakistani Consulate.

Abhay's smile breaks into a chuckle.

                    ABHAY
          Why would they hire an Indian?

                    PRIYANKA
          I'm Pakistani.

Abhay's eyes narrow with confusion.

                    ABHAY
          But... Priyanka is a Hindu name.
          You are Hindu, aren't you?

                    PRIYANKA
          Hindu, yes, from Pakistan. Which
          makes me a Pakistani, genius.

                    ABHAY
          You are kidding, right? Tell me you
          are kidding.

                    PRIYANKA
          No. What's the problem?

Abhay's jaw tightens.

                              ABHAY
                    Shit.


**EXT. UNITED NATIONS - DAY**

MONTAGE OF UNITED NATIONS BUILDING. A DARK PRISON.

It stands as a forbidding structure as CARS drive by.


**INT. KITCHEN - DAY**

Priyanka enters. Abhay follows. As she makes coffee --

                         PRIYANKA
                    In these times, here in America, do
                    you really have to be so
                    parochial...? What difference does
                    it make if I'm Pakistani?

Abhay sees a PAKISTANI FLAG on the refrigerator door.

                         ABHAY
                    You don't understand. Pri, I can't
                    be with a Pakistani...

                         PRIYANKA
                    That's so lame. You are so lame.

                         ABHAY
                    I just... I thought you were
                    Indian.

                         PRIYANKA
                    And I thought you were a pretty
                    cool guy.
                         (beat)
                    Guess we were both wrong.

                         ABHAY
                    I work for India's Home Ministry...

                         PRIYANKA
                    And they don't allow you to have
                    Pakistani friends?

                         ABHAY
                    We'd be more than friends.
                         (beat)
                    The Home Ministry is responsible
                    for maintenance of the country's
                    internal security...

PRIYANKA
I know what the Home Ministry is
for.

ABHAY
You are a consular officer. Our
relationship would never pass
scrutiny.

PRIYANKA
Scrutiny? Do you see me as some
threat to your country's internal
security?

ABHAY
It doesn't matter what I think, or
say or do. You will be classified
as a threat. By my people, and by
yours too.

PRIYANKA
Would you agree with them?

ABHAY
Of course not.

Beat.

ABHAY
Pri, my parents were both killed in
the two thousand five bombings in
Delhi. Okay? I swore that day, as a
sixteen year old boy, to protect my
people...

PRIYANKA
I'm sorry about your parents. I
really am.
     (beat)
Abhay, I'm not a threat to you,
your people, or anyone. That's the
truth.

ABHAY
Truth doesn't matter. Perception is
everything.

PRIYANKA
You are right. Perception is
everything. You and I, here in
America, are perceived as a threat
by many. Truth doesn't matter to
them either.

Priyanka puts on her HEADBAND. She grabs her RUNNING
HEADPHONES.

> ABHAY
> Pri...

> PRIYANKA
> (soft, not angry)
> Please. Don't call me that.
> (puts her headphones on)
> Look, I'm going for a run. I'll see
> you when I get back. If you are
> still here.

ABHAY watches her walk past, wincing at the sound of the
front door being slammed shut.

## INT. KITCHEN - DAY

Abhay, upset. Struggling with what he needs to do.

> FADE TO BLACK.

## EXT. UNITED NATIONS - DAY

Abhay looks at his workplace. Trying to decide if he should
call Priyanka or not. As he wonders --

## EXT. PARK - DAY

Priyanka is out jogging. She gets a call. She stops to
answer.

> ABHAY
> Hi, Pri.

Priyanka says nothing. Waiting for him to make the move.

> ABHAY
> I love you.

## EXT. SIDEWALK - UNITED NATIONS - DAY

Abhay listens. And Priyanka says exactly what he wants to
hear.

> PRIYANKA
> I love you too.

He smiles

                    ABHAY
          I'll see you soon, Pri.

He hangs up.

**EXT. PARK - DAY**

Priyanka, a slight smile on her lips, hangs up. Then,
suddenly thinking of something, she dials a number.

Is she calling Abhay back? But her tone says no.

                    PRIYANKA
          I got him.
               (listens)
          Operation N2 is a go.

Priyanka hangs up the phone. Looking pleased with herself.

OFF PRIYANKA

                                        CUT TO BLACK.


                        **THE END**

# Chapter Four

## About "Sunflower/Soul" and "Tulip/Rock"

TULIP/ROCK came into existence without a script—an unconventional path for a film. While on a family trip to Chandigarh, India, I was determined to visit Shimla, a nearby hill station. Despite heavy rain and the potential and realized risk of falling rocks, I made the solo trip, promising my wife I'd turn back if the road felt too dangerous.

Armed only with my iPhone, I began capturing moments with no idea of the story. As I filmed, an emotion surfaced, then the faint outline of a narrative.

Only in post-production did I write and assemble the script. Structured as voiceover, it takes a form very different from a traditional screenplay.

The result was deeply personal—and drew mixed feedback. One festival reviewer wrote, "While very poetic and emotionally poised, the film feels more like a personal apology than a cinematic experience. Some shots are strong and wonderful, but others lack purpose, creating a discrepancy in visual style."

Not long after that unenthusiastic review, TULIP/ROCK won first prize in a film magazine's short-film contest, judged by acclaimed cinematographer Michael Goi, ASC.

I've learned to meet both rejection and success with equanimity.

Filmmaking isn't about perfection; it's about creating with the tools, skills, and opportunities I have. Each project reflects my capabilities, limitations, and current level of craft—and that's enough.

SUNFLOWER/SOUL was born under different, yet equally profound, circumstances.

After my mother's passing, I returned to India, navigating grief. Unsure whether I was using filmmaking as an escape, I ultimately felt her guiding presence urging me to create. I shot the film on my iPhone, but it took two years before I could return to the material. In doing so, I found solace—and a deeper understanding of how my father had coped with the loss of his own parents.

✱✱✱

These films are pieces of my heart and soul, created in intensely personal moments. Freed from all filmmaking rules and processes. I had no crew. No cast. Just whatever was in front of me.

I hope they mean something to you as they have to me.

# TULIP/ROCK

                    NIKHIL (V.O)
I am not afraid of heights. I have
a fear of falling.
It's called Ba-so-phobia.
     (beat)
I remember the day basophobia
entered my life
I was at the JAKHOO TEMPLE which is
at the top of the highest peak in
Shimla.
ON THAT DAY, I suffered the worst
fall of my life. The fall from her
grace.
She… was my rock, but she was as
fragile as a Tulip. She… thought
she was safe with me
She… trusted me
ON THAT DAY,, I destroyed her… when
I confessed that I had kissed
another woman.
It was nothing, I said
Just a drunken kiss, I said It
meant nothing, I said,
I was wrong.
It meant everything to her.
     (beat)
In the presence of Hanuman, the
monkey god, she made me promise I
would not follow her. Then she ran.
She ran down a thousand steps.
She ran so far away from me while I
stood still… keeping a promise, to
make up for breaking another.
     (beat)
ON THAT DAY, a butterfly flapped
its wings somewhere in the world
And a rock shifted its weight at
the top of a hill
Hurtling down towards her car Which
swerved to avoid a collision,
Only to drive off the road, and
tumble down the hill Choosing one
death over another for her
     (beat)
In her final moments, maybe she
forgave my selfish, self-centered,

self-absorbed nature. But I will
never forgive myself. I cannot
forgive myself.
I have grown older. But she'll
forever remain young.
One day, I will join her. Maybe she
will forgive me. If she does,
maybe, I'll find the courage to
fall in love again…

**<u>THE END</u>**

# SUNFLOWER/SOUL

**EXT. BACKYARD GARDEN - INDIA - DAY**

A DOG TEARS UP a large tree leaf. A hand comes in and picks up a part of the leaf and hands it to the dog.

WE HEAR DISTANT EXPLOSIONS -- CAR CHASE -- GUNFIRE --

**INT. HALL - DAY**

And we are listening to an ACTION SEQUENCE from a film on an UNSEEN TV that blares in the background.

CLOSE ON: VIJAY (40s), his head recently shaved.

Vijay holds TV REMOTE in his hand. He drops it to pick up a phone -- wanting to make a call.

**EXT. ROOFTOP - DAY**

A TRAIN THUNDERS BY -- as Vijay watches. He gets a call. His face lights up as he answers.

> VIJAY
> Hey. How's it going? I was waiting
> for your call.
> (beat)
> Nothing. Just watching trains. Like
> I used to when I was a kid. My
> happy place.
> (beat)
> I'm going to go check out my
> grandfather's place in the Old City
> today. Doing my farewell rounds, I
> guess before I head back home.
> Khushi, it's been a long separation
> for us. I know it's been hard for
> you to not see me for two whole
> years. But... just a few more days
> and then I'm back. Are you looking
> forward to it? I can't wait. Khush?
> Are you there? Hello? Hello?

**INT. TRAIN - DAY**

Vijay is seated by the window in a train. The urban

landscape of the city zips by.

**INT. AUTO - DAY**

Vijay rides an auto through the OLD CITY streets.

>            VIJAY (V.O.)
> Everything changes. Nothing lasts
> forever. Seems true enough. Right?
> But if that's true, what does that
> actually mean? If everything
> changes, doesn't love change too?
> If nothing lasts forever, then love
> won't either. Right?

**INT. IRANI CAFE - NIGHT**

Vijay with his friend, PRASAD (40s). They drink from a cup
of Irani chai.

>            PRASAD
> Why so philosophical, boss? Let it
> all go. Some problem with Khushi?

>            VIJAY
> She's just being... distant. Thoda
> cut off ho gayi.

>            PRASAD
> So you left her alone for two years
> to take care of your dad. Of
> course, she'll be upset, right?

>            VIJAY
> She could have come with me.

>            PRASAD
> Uska bhi job hai. You can't expect
> her to just give it up.

>            VIJAY
> I know. I know.

>            PRASAD
> What did you do today?

>            VIJAY
> I went to see Ajoba's house.

>            PRASAD
> Old city? Wow. Akele?

                    VIJAY
          Yeah.


**EXT. OLD CITY - DAY**

Vijay travels to CHARMINAR in a car and then stands outside
a GATE of a house. He makes a VIDEO CALL to Khushi.

                    VIJAY
          Hey.

She's detached, polite, but there's kindness in there.

                    KHUSHI (V.O.)
               (on phone)
          Hi.

                    VIJAY
          I can't see you. Is your camera on?

                    KHUSHI
          No.

                    VIJAY
          Turn it on.

                    KHUSHI
          No...

                    VIJAY
          I want to see your face...

                    KHUSHI
          Vijay, I'm not going to turn my
          camera on.

His smile falters at her tone.

                    VIJAY
          Okay. I... that's okay. How are
          you?

                    KHUSHI
          Fine.

                    VIJAY
          Our call got disconnected last
          time. I tried calling back...

                    KHUSHI
          I was busy. I have to work, you
          know.

Vijay inhales sharply. Gathers himself.

                    VIJAY
          What went wrong between us, Khush?

                    KHUSHI
          You left, Vijay. That's what
          happened. Don't you remember?

                    VIJAY
          I came here to take care of my
          dad...

                    KHUSHI
          And? When I asked you to
          reconsider...? When I asked you to
          explore other options...?

                    VIJAY
          He's my dad.

                    KHUSHI
          And I'm your wife. Or maybe not.

                    VIJAY
          He needed me.

                    KHUSHI
          He needed help. It didn't have to
          be yours. It didn't have to be for
          two long years.

                    VIJAY
          Khush...

                    KHUSHI
          I filed for our divorce.

                    VIJAY
          What?

                    KHUSHI
          You'll have a month to contest it.
          I hope you don't. So I can file for
          a default judgement. Soon as the
          judge signs, our marriage will be
          over.

                    VIJAY
          Khush, why are doing this? Why now?

                    KHUSHI
          You don't need to come back for me,
          Vijay.

                    VIJAY
          Don't do this. We are going to be
          together.

                    KHUSHI
          After two years of living like
          strangers? When you left, you were
          so angry, you tore up our wedding
          certificate. Our wedding
          photographs. Every single last one
          of them.

                    VIJAY
          I am sorry. I was wrong. That was
          so wrong. I know I was wrong.

                    KHUSHI
          Then you know why I'm doing this.

                    VIJAY
          We can start over...

                    KHUSHI
          I have to go to work.

                    VIJAY
          Don't hang up on me. Wait.

Khushi hangs up. Vijay stares at the phone.

**EXT. TRAIN STATION - INDIA - DAY**

Vijay sits -- mask on. Stares at the oncoming train.

Vijay watches several trains come and go.

**INT. AUTO - INDIA - NIGHT**

Vijay sits in the backseat of an auto.

**EXT. TANKBUND - INDIA - NIGHT**

Vijay on the phone.

                    KHUSHI (V.O.)
          Vijay, I have to go.

                    VIJAY
          Khush, we can make this work. You
          know we can...

> KHUSHI
> I've been seeing someone.

> VIJAY
> What?

> KHUSHI
> I'm tired of all the lies and
> secrets with everyone I know. With
> you. I'm tired of you. I'm tired of
> your issues. Your problems. Your
> dreams. Your ambitions. Your films.
> Your... everything. I'm tired of
> this life when I'm with you. Let me
> go, Vijay. Just let me go
> peacefully. Stop tearing me apart.
> I can't take it anymore. All I want
> is to just be with Adam.

As Vijay looks out over Tankbund.

A MASSIVE EXPLOSION over the water results in a fireball.

THEN -- he turns to see GUNFIRE ERUPT in the darkness.

A NIGHTMARISH EXPERIENCE as SEVERAL MORE EXPLOSIONS resound
in the night around the city.

CLOSE ON VIJAY --

SQUEALS / TRAFFIC CRASHES / SCREAMS

And then: A BULLET HOLE in Vijay's forehead as he's SHOT
between the eyes.

> CUT TO:


**INT. HALL - DAY**

Vijay -- on the stone floor -- his eyes FLY OPEN. Next to
him, a BOTTLE OF WHISKY. A glass. As he sits up, he pushes
the whisky bottle to the side.

He leans against a wall. A SMILE OF ACCEPTANCE touches his
lips even as a SINGLE TEAR rolls down his cheek.

## THE END

# Chapter Five

## About "Liberty"

LIBERTY is an unproduced script that found recognition on Coverfly, consistently ranking in the Top 10 Thrillers for an extended period. It channels my enduring love of Shakespeare and my ambition to weave his timeless language into a new narrative.

The script began as an attempt to honor Shakespeare's style while reimagining his words in a different context. I combed through his works, carefully selecting lines that aligned with my story's intent. It felt like scavenging at times—but when you're drawing from one of the greatest storytellers of all time, what you build can still feel extraordinary, even within the limits of your current craft. I approached the work with humility—as a student eager to learn from the master.

LIBERTY is more than a standalone piece; it's the foundation for a larger story world. The concept has since grown into ELiRiUM, an epic TV series that blends futuristic fantasy and sci-fi with Shakespearean tragedy at its heart.

LIBERTY has been recognized as a semifinalist in the WeScreenplay screenwriting contest, and its big-sister project, ELiRiUM, has benefited from development workshops with industry veterans Nina Fiore and John Herrera (The Handmaid's Tale). ELiRiUM is still evolving as a TV pilot and isn't yet ready to share, but I'm hopeful it will grow into a series worth watching.

LIBERTY remains a script I dream of bringing to life. Regardless of the projects it inspired, it carries a tone and feeling I'd love to see on screen.

For now, I hope you enjoy reading the script.

# LIBERTY

**INT. TRIBAL CEREMONIAL ROOM - NIGHT**

Its a dark room. Roving beams of light reveal TRIBAL ARTIFACTS and artwork on the walls.

TRIBAL ELECTRONIC DANCE MUSIC plays in the background.

Beams of light reveal TRIBAL HANDGUNS held by hands adorned with tribal jewelry. Each gun, distinctive, yet all display a symbol made of the letters "Hg" and the symbol for Mercury.

The hands thrust the guns into the air to the beat of the music.

Its a tribal ceremony.

Each wrist has a skin tight GLOWING LIGHT BAND, under which a tattoo that reads "LIBERTY".

A mix of MALE and FEMALE VOICES take an oath in unison.

> VOICES
> Let fame, that all hunt after in
> their lives, grace us in death.
> Tell me not of fear. We were born
> to die. Give me strength to free
> Aquitaine from this present shame.
> Tyrant Capulet, I shoot thee.
> Tyrant Montague, I shoot thee. A
> plague o' both your houses.

The guns fire twice towards the ceiling. BLAM! BLAM!

WE LOOK UP to see we are under the OPEN STARLIT SKY. This room has no ceiling, and is in fact, just four walls erected in the middle of WILDERNESS.

In the night sky, we see TWO MOONS, a smaller one orbits a larger one underscoring the fact that although familiar to us, this is NOT OUR WORLD.

**INT. TELEVISION STUDIO - DAY**

We are in a studio where a NEWS ANCHOR, 30s, interviews PRESIDENT CHARLES MONTAGUE. Monitors behind and to his side display the broadcast signal.

With them are TWO GUESTS - one male, one female, both in their 50s.

All are immaculately dressed in business suits.

ON THE MONITOR: Close up of the President with a title at the bottom of the screen

TITLE: "PRESIDENT CHARLES MONTAGUE - UNITED CORPORATIONS OF NAVARRE"

> PRESIDENT
> Aquitaine is bound to us.

> NEWS ANCHOR
> But, most esteemed greatness, will you hear the dialogue that the two learned men have compiled...

> PRESIDENT
> Hear two learned men armed in arguments? No. Let them gaze upon my men-at-arms.

The President waves at TWO ARMED GUARDS, towering, very intimidating, standing to the side.

> PRESIDENT
> The King of Verona owes a hundred thousand crowns disbursed by me in his wars, in surety of the which, Aquitaine is bound to us.

> NEWS ANCHOR
> The King has produced acquittances for such a sum...

The anchor hands the President a LEGAL DOCUMENT.

The President scans key phrases. "RIGHT IN AQUITAINE", "PAYMENT RECEIVED", "FULLY REPAID"... and with TWO SIGNATURES at the bottom.

"CHARLES MONTAGUE" - PRESIDENT, UNITED CORPORATIONS OF NAVARRE

"GHALIB CAPULET" - KING, CORPORATE FEDERATION OF VERONA

The witness space is signed by the "WCC : WORLD CORPORATE COURT".

                                              CUT TO:


**INT. CAR - DAY**

PRINCE ROMEO MONTAGUE, 30s, the President's son, watches TV in the car.

He wears a full-sleeved business shirt and jeans. He pulls out a SILVER BRACELET hidden under the sleeve on his left hand.

Looped on the bracelet is a SYCAMORE LEAF shaped in metal, and on it a single letter. The letter is 'J'.

INTERCUT - STUDIO / CAR'S TV MONITOR

                    NEWS ANCHOR
              It is your writing, and here is
              your name.

The anchor ploughs on while the President considers the document he is holding.

                    NEWS ANCHOR
              The King of Verona will surely hold
              fair friendship with you.

The anchor turns to his two guests excited with an idea.

                    NEWS ANCHOR
              The President, and his son, Romeo,
              could be our men of peace.

The guests point at the President and the anchor turns to see the President has set fire to the document.

                    PRESIDENT
              Peace. I hate the word.

                    NEWS ANCHOR
              War. In that word's death.

The President throws the burnt document away and stands up.

                    PRESIDENT
              Be quiet, or I'll make you quiet.

The President turns back to the CAMERA.

>           PRESIDENT
> Befall, what will befall. My son,
> Romeo and I... we will never give
> up our right in Aquitaine. We will
> prepare for war.

The guests get up and leave.

## INT. CAR - DAY

The Prince watches.

A sign flashes on the screen.

"CORPORATION VS CORPORATION - A CIVIL WAR"

Then an attractive SALESWOMAN appears holding a piece of copper shaped into a bar.

>           SALESWOMAN
> Do you hear? Do you see? Civil war,
> it shall be. News indeed. If so,
> our copper buys better. Thou
> shouldst have it to buy. Buy, buy,
> buy!

Romeo sees his friend and protector, BIRON, 30s, walking towards the car, holding DRINKS.

He turns the TV off and hides the silver bracelet under this shirt sleeve.

Biron opens the passenger side door and sits. Offers the Prince one of the drinks. Prince nods a no.

>           BIRON
> You love her.

>           ROMEO
> You are deceived, I do not.

>           BIRON
> I'll read the ode you have writ...

Biron pulls out a piece of paper from the glove compartment and reads -

>           BIRON
>      (faux dramatic imitation)
> I would forget her, but a fever she
> reigns in my blood and will
> remember'd be...

Romeo snatches the paper. Stuffs it in his pocket. Biron
laughs.

> BIRON
> Tell me. Who is it that you love?

> ROMEO
> Go home! Adieu.

> BIRON
> No, my good lord, I have sworn to
> stay with you.

Romeo shakes his head. Good friends here.

> BIRON
> Where is your lady?

> ROMEO
> Half a mile...

> BIRON
> Half a mile to meet some mistress
> fine.

> ROMEO
> No mistress. Princess Juliet. She
> comes in secret from Verona.

Beat.

> BIRON
> She seeks to undo us...

> ROMEO
> Not true.

> BIRON
> What is the purpose of her coming?

> ROMEO
> Aquitaine.

Biron lets out a soft whistle.

> BIRON
> Vainly comes the admired Princess
> hither. Juliet Capulet is the only
> daughter of your father's great
> enemy. The President...

> ROMEO
> ...must not know.

They exchange a glance. Biron nods.

> BIRON
> Your grace need not fear.

Romeo starts the car and pulls out. They both look ahead.
The mood now is serious. No more jovial conversation.

## EXT. COUNTRY ROAD - DAY

The sedan drives away on a deserted country road. Away from
the distant SKYLINE of the city of NAVARRE.

## INT. SUV - DAY

BOYETTE, a young woman in her late 30s, turns to look at her
passenger, PRINCESS JULIET, 30s.

She looks in the rear view mirror and sees the Prince's car
approaching in the distance.

Boyette hands her a gun.

> BOYETTE
> This shall slay them both.

Juliet takes the gun and looks it over.

> JULIET
> I am the shooter?

> BOYETTE
> You are the shooter. And who is
> your deer?

> JULIET
> Romeo. The Prince of Navarre.

> BOYETTE
> Excellent.

Boyette sees the car, now much closer, in the rear view
mirror. Juliet puts the gun down on the dashboard.

> JULIET
> I know him, Boyette.

> BOYETTE
> Know?

> JULIET
> Know.

                    BOYETTE
How canst thou know the President's
son? Our foe?

                    JULIET
At a marriage feast between Lord
Perigort and the beauteous heir of
Jacques Falconbridge solemnized in
Normandy saw I this Romeo.

                    BOYETTE
Saw?

                    JULIET
Saw.

                    BOYETTE
Now I know his reason to meet
you... I should have ask'd you that
before.

                    JULIET
I am in love too.

                    BOYETTE
Romeo is beloved. Juliet loves
again.
        (turns on Juliet)
Romeo is a Montague, our foe, a
villain that is hither come in
spite. Thou consort'st with a
villain.

                    JULIET
Thou know'st him not.

Boyette looks up at the mirror and sees the car pull to a
stop. She picks up the gun and holds it out for Juliet.

                    BOYETTE
Take Romeo's life! You must do it.
Consider who the king, your father,
sends. To whom he sends.

Juliet takes the gun, then places it on the center console.

                    JULIET
I have another way.

Juliet opens the door and steps out. Boyette grabs the gun
and steps out.

**EXT. OPEN CLEARING - DESOLATE GRASSY AREA - DAY**

Boyette holsters the gun in the small of her back.

The car pulls to a stop and Biron and Romeo exit to face Juliet and Boyette standing near their car.

Romeo steps forward as does Juliet and they meet in the center. Biron and Boyette stay back near the vehicles.

ROMEO AND JULIET

> ROMEO
> Fair Princess... welcome.

Juliet holds her hand out to Romeo which he kisses gently.

> ROMEO
> Did not I dance with you in
> Normandy once?

Juliet flashes him an angry look. Then, slaps him and stalks off. Romeo chases after her.

Juliet turns on Romeo and hisses quietly so that Biron and Boyette can't hear.

> JULIET
> Did not I dance with you in
> Normandy once?

> ROMEO
> I know you did.

> JULIET
> How needless was it then to ask the
> question.

> ROMEO
> You must not be so quick.

> JULIET
> Then don't spur me with such
> questions.

Juliet grabs his hand, and hurls him to the ground in a JUDO-like move.

> ROMEO
> OW.

Biron tries to take a step forward but is stopped by Boyette's look.

Juliet kneels next to Romeo. She sees the bracelet on his hand and the leaf with the letter 'J'.

> JULIET
> J... For Jaquenetta?

> ROMEO
> Your wit's too hot, it speeds too fast; 'twill tire.

> JULIET
> Not till it leave the rider in the mire.

She touches the metal sycamore leaf. She pulls out her necklace looped around which is a metal sycamore leaf, exactly like the one Romeo has. Except, on hers the letter is 'R'.

> JULIET
> 'R' for Romeo.

They smile at each other. She gives him a hand and stands him up.

He moves to kiss her. She stops him.

> JULIET
> Resolve me in my suit. Surrender up Aquitaine.

> ROMEO
> Juliet, your father, the King, owes my father, the President, hundred thousand crowns...

> JULIET
> You do the king, my father, too much wrong, and wrong the reputation of your name, in so unseeming to confess receipt of that which hath so faithfully been paid.

> ROMEO
> I do protest I never heard of it.

Juliet glares at him.

> JULIET
> Then leave.

> ROMEO
> For your fair sake have we

    neglected time...

             JULIET
    I received your letters, full of
    love.

Boyette yells out from a distance.

             BOYETTE
    Gentle Romeo, we must have a dance.

             ROMEO
    You may not come, fair princess,
    within my gates... it may do much
    danger.

             JULIET
    I cannot go home. And this field-
    bed is too cold for me to sleep...

Biron comes up.

             BIRON
    Excuse me, Princess.

He leads the Prince away.

             BIRON
    What great men have been in love?

             ROMEO
    What?

             BIRON
    Answer me.

Romeo decides to go along.

             ROMEO
    Hercules.

             BIRON
    Sweet Hercules! Name more.

             ROMEO
    Samson.

             BIRON
    He was a man of good carriage.
    Carried the town gates on his back
    like a porter. He was in love!

Biron throws up a high five. Romeo glares in return. Biron
simmers down and whispers.

                         BIRON
             We could withdraw unto some private
             place.

                         ROMEO
             Whose private place?

Biron hesitates and responds with a grin.

                         BIRON
             A fair lady, my lord.

                         ROMEO
             Rosaline.

Biron lowers his head.

                         BIRON
             Yes, my lord.

MEANWHILE, NEAR JULIET AND BOYETTE

Juliet looks defeated. Boyette whispers to her handing her
the gun out of sight of Romeo and Biron.

                         BOYETTE
             Slay Romeo. Romeo has most power to
             do most harm.

                         JULIET
             I lack power to move. Ancient
             damnation!

                         BOYETTE
             Time is very short...

Juliet pushes the gun back to her.

                         BOYETTE
             You will not, then?

Juliet shakes her head - "no".

                         BOYETTE
             I will do it without fear or doubt.

                         JULIET
             Hold. I do spy a kind of hope.

Boyette is shocked to hear this and lowers the gun.

Juliet and Romeo lock eyes, full of longing.

**INT. CAR - DAY**

Romeo and Juliet in the backseat.

Biron drives, and Boyette rides shotgun.

**EXT. OPEN CLEARING - DESOLATE GRASSY AREA - DAY**

Car exits the clearing. SUV left behind.

**INT. CAR - DAY**

Biron drives, and Boyette rides shotgun.

Romeo and Juliet in the backseat.

Boyette watches them for a moment in the rear-view mirror catching Juliet smile coyly at Romeo.

**EXT. CITYSCAPE - DAY**

BMW turns around a mountain and in the distance the gleaming SKYLINE of a city is revealed.

**INT. CAR - DAY**

RADIO is tuned to a PANEL DISCUSSION.

> MALE PANELIST
> Verona, Navarre... two of the
> fairest stars, run by two
> households both alike in dignity.

> FEMALE PANELIST
> The King and the President.

> MALE PANELIST
> And there's Aquitaine...

> FEMALE PANELIST
> This jewel with rebellious subjects
> who shout "liberty".

> MALE PANELIST
> (scoffs)
> Liberty from what?

> FEMALE PANELIST
> Enemies to peace.

                    MALE PANELIST
          Beasts, who have disturb'd the
          quiet of our streets.

                   FEMALE PANELIST
          Their lives will pay the forfeit of
          peace, no matter if its the
          President or the King who wins
          Aquitaine.

Boyette looks thoughtful. Her gaze moves to the GPS SCREEN.

On it, THREE PLACES are displayed. "NAVARRE", "VERONA" and
"AQUITAINE."

Her interest slowly goes towards that one name on the screen
"AQUITAINE".


**EXT. STREET - DAY**

The car pulls to a stop on the side of the road. Everyone
piles out of the car. Biron leads the way, crossing the road
towards a building.


**EXT. BUILDING - DAY**

The sign on the building reads "SYCAMORE DAZE"

Biron opens the door. Everyone enters.


**INT. UNDERGROUND DANCE CLUB - DAY**

Door opens and the foursome enter.

Bright flashing lights strobe away the darkness. A SONG
plays to a crisp electronic beats.

                      CHORUS
          A lover's eyes will gaze an eagle
          blind;
          A lover's ear will hear the lowest
          sound;
          When Love speaks, the voice of all
          the gods
          Makes heaven drowsy with the
          harmony...

The Chorus moves into a verse.

                     SINGER (O.S.)
          All men love,

```
               A Lover's Eye,
               All men love,
               A Lover's Tongue
               Love is first learned
               In a Lady's Eye...
```

The beats blare, distort, syncopate as...

                    BIRON
          Quick recreation granted!

Biron catches Romeo's eyes looks at him serious-like. Then -

                    BIRON
          Romeo! Madman! Lover!

Romeo flips him the bird. Biron grabs TWO DRINKS from a
SERVER who appears with a TRAY OF DRINKS.

                    BIRON
          We men are men. We love our merry
          hours.

Romeo smiles at Juliet, and she lets the hint of a smile
dance on her lips.

                    ROMEO
          We will dance.

                    JULIET
          More than once.

Romeo and Juliet breakaway.

Boyette watches them go. Biron slides up next to her and
offers her a drink.

                    BIRON
          Biron.

Boyette ignores him.

                    BIRON
          I desire your name.

                    BOYETTE
          I have but one for myself.

                    BIRON
          Who's daughter art thou?

                    BOYETTE
          My mother's I have heard.

                    BIRON
               (to himself)
          Mad wench.

                    BOYETTE
          What did you whisper?

                    BIRON
          That thou art a most sweet lady.

Boyette watches Juliet and Romeo kiss. Biron watches also.

                    BIRON
          If my observation, which very
          seldom lies... deceive me not now,
          Romeo is infected. With that which
          we lovers call love...

                    BOYETTE
          Thou art deceived.

Boyette can barely watch them kiss and grabs the drink from
Biron and downs it.

                    BIRON
          I... I seek a wife! A woman, ay.
          And by heaven, one that will do the
          deed!

                    BOYETTE
          You are a gentleman and a gamester,
          sir.

                    BIRON
          I confess both. They are both the
          varnish of a complete man.

                    BOYETTE
          With that face.

                    BIRON
          I love thee.

                    BOYETTE
          So I heard you say.

                    BIRON
          And so...

                    BOYETTE
          And so, farewell.

Boyette tries to leave, but Biron holds her wrist.

                         BIRON
              A dance?

Boyette glares at him and he lets go of her arm. Boyette
walks away.

Biron shifts attention to a VOLUPTUOUS WOMAN who smiles and
waves at him.

ROSALINE, 30s, walks over.

                         BIRON
                    Rosaline, we must withdraw unto
                    some private place. Here all eyes
                    gaze upon us.

Rosaline nods.


**EXT. ELEVATOR - DAY**

Rosaline leads Romeo, Biron, Boyette and Juliet to an
elevator. They get in. The doors close.


**EXT. ELEVATOR - DIFFERENT FLOOR - DAY**

Doors open and the trio walks out. Rosaline leads them to a
door and opens it. They walk in.

Rosaline closes the door. Waits a moment. Walks away.


**INT. PRINCESS'S SUITE - DAY**

Romeo and Juliet stand close together. Biron is on his
phone, sees Boyette watching Romeo and Juliet. He walks over
to her.

Romeo and Juliet enter a room and they close the door.

Biron strokes Boyette's hair.

                         BIRON
                    (to Boyette)
                    O, let us embrace, sweet lover.

Boyette spins and PUNCHES Biron. She grabs him by the balls
and SHOVES him against the wall. Then grabbing him by the
hair, she walks him to the door and shoves him out.

                         BOYETTE
              Whoreson.

Boyette slams the door shut.

> BIRON (O.S.)
> A fever you reign in my blood... I
> love thee.

Boyette cracks a smile. Briefly. Very briefly.

Boyette moves closer towards the room. She gently pushes the door open and sees -

Romeo and Juliet kiss.

> JULIET
> Surrender up Aquitaine.

> ROMEO
> I surrender all that is mine...

And he kisses her. She pushes him away.

> ROMEO
> O, I am yours, and all that I
> possess.

Now she lets him kiss her and push her down on the bed.

Boyette can't take it anymore and looks away.

> BOYETTE
> (quietly)
> Well, we were born to die.

She raises her gun. But can't pull the trigger. Lowers it.


**INT. PRESIDENT'S CHAMBERS - DAY**

An OLD LADY walks in with a SHADOWY FIGURE into the President's chambers.

> OLD LADY
> This maid from Verona here comes
> with yourself to speak.

The President looks up and gestures for her to be allowed in.

The figure steps into light. It's Boyette!

She bows.

> BOYETTE
> My lord. I bring news in the secret

night.

                    PRESIDENT
          Speak.

                    BOYETTE
          Juliet here comes in embassy to
          speak about surrender up of
          Aquitaine with your son, Romeo.

                    PRESIDENT
          With my son?

                    BOYETTE
          Yes, my lord.

The President's blaze with anger. He begins to pace.

                    PRESIDENT
          Continue.

                    BOYETTE
          They have the plague. In their
          hearts it lies. My eyes saw his
          eyes enchanted with gazes.

The President grabs Boyette by her neck and shoves her
against the wall.

                    PRESIDENT
          Thou art an old love monger.

                    BOYETTE
          I speak in words that which my eye
          hath disclosed.

                    PRESIDENT
          Thou speakest skillfully.

                    BOYETTE
          I only have made a mouth of my eye
          by adding a tongue which I know
          will not lie.

                    PRESIDENT
          Where is the Princess?

                    BOYETTE
          What would you with the Princess?

                    PRESIDENT
          Nothing but peace and gentle
          visitation.

The President brandishes his gun. Boyette hesitates.

                    BOYETTE
          I know not, sir.

                    PRESIDENT
          Then find out. Come back again. You
          will be rewarded.

The President lets go of her neck. Boyette leaves.

The President hits a button on his communication intercom.

                    PRESIDENT
          Find my son. Find Romeo.


**INT. PRESIDENT'S CHAMBERS - DAY**

Romeo opens the door and enters. The President smokes a
cigar.

                    ROMEO
          Good morrow, father.

                    PRESIDENT
          My dear son. Where hast thou been?

Romeo sits. The President hands him a cigar and lights it
for him.

                    ROMEO
          Underneath the grove of sycamore
          that westward rooteth from the
          city's side.

The President arches his eyebrows.

                    PRESIDENT
          You lie.

The President takes a puff of his cigar, and smiles coldly
at Romeo.

                    ROMEO
          I understand you not.

                    PRESIDENT
          Where is the Princess?

Romeo exhales slowly. Carefully.

                    ROMEO
          Spakest thou of Juliet?

                    PRESIDENT
That's my good son. Where is your
conceal'd lady?


                    ROMEO
My lord. I am in love.


                    PRESIDENT
Love. These violent delights have
violent ends and in their triumph
die, like fire and powder, which as
they kiss consume.


                    ROMEO
It is enough I may but call her
mine, my lord.


                    PRESIDENT
Compare her face with some that I
shall show, and I will make thee
think thy swan a crow. Aquitaine is
bound to us. When she shall
challenge this, you will kill her.


                    ROMEO
Peace, my lord.


                    PRESIDENT
I hate the word. We will be the
beginners of this fray. What day is
this?


                    ROMEO
Monday...


                    PRESIDENT
Monday! Ha ha! Well, Wednesday is
too soon. O' Thursday let it be to
set this ancient quarrel new
abroach. Will you be ready? Do you
like this haste?


                    ROMEO
No, father...


                    PRESIDENT
The Princess comes to hunt here.
And thou standest as her prey.
Aquitaine is, and will remain,
bound to us.


                    ROMEO
Then plainly know my heart's dear
love is set on the fair Princess.

As mine on hers, so hers is set on
mine...

                    PRESIDENT
          Hold your tongue. Aquitaine is my
          crown jewel. You are my son. She is
          thine enemy.

The President gathers himself. The genial smile returns. He
pats Romeo on his shoulder.

                    PRESIDENT
          Talk no more of this matter. My
          son.

The President extinguishes his cigar in the ashtray. Romeo
leaves.

## INT. PRINCE'S ROOM - BED - NIGHT

Romeo and Juliet kiss. Postcoital bliss.

                    ROMEO
          Did I not dance with you last
          night?

                    JULIET
          More than once.

They laugh. She nibbles at his ear.

                    JULIET
          Resolve me in my suit.

                    ROMEO
          I will do it. For my queen.

He takes off HIS RING and puts it on her finger. Its LOOSE.
She laughs. He makes a sad face. Cute.

They kiss.

                    JULIET
          My lord.

                    ROMEO
          My lady.

And they kiss again.

**INT. PRINCESS'S SUITE - BEDROOM - DAY**

Juliet enters with a smile and a bounce. Boyette grabs her by the wrist.

> BOYETTE
> Juliet, do as sworn to do.

> JULIET
> Hold me not. Let me go.

> BOYETTE
> Subscribe to your deepest oaths.
> Slay that villain Romeo.

> JULIET
> Blister'd be thy tongue.

Boyette sees the ring on her finger.

> BOYETTE
> What's this? What's this?

> JULIET
> God join'ed my heart and Romeo's...

Boyette shocked, is frozen for only a moment. She pulls Juliet closer and kisses her.

Juliet, shocked, manages to push Boyette away, end the kiss.

> JULIET
> Good lord, Boyette. If anyone sees
> thee, they will murder thee.

> BOYETTE
> There lies more peril in thine eye.
> My heart is in thy breast. If my
> heart's dear love...

> JULIET
> I will away tonight. With Romeo.

> BOYETTE
> My life were better ended, Juliet.

> JULIET
> I care not.

Juliet exits the bedroom.

Boyette breaks down. She cries. Through her tears, her face hardens. She picks up the phone and dials a number. Her call is answered.

                    BOYETTE
          Mr. President, I have found the
          Princess.


## INT. COFFEE SHOP - DAY

Romeo and Biron drink coffee.

                    ROMEO
          I from this must fly. Heaven is
          where Juliet lives.

                    BIRON
          Thou runn'st away? I see that
          madmen have no ears.

                    ROMEO
          Thou canst not speak of that thou
          dost not feel.

Beat.

                    ROMEO
          Will you go with me?

                    BIRON
          Yes, my lord.


## INT. PRINCESS'S SUITE - NIGHT

The DOORBELL RINGS. Juliet, thinking its Romeo, rushes to
open the door.

Its the President. He walks in, as TWO ARMED GUARDS stand on
either side of him.

Juliet walks backwards.

                    JULIET
          Boyette!

Juliet turns and sees Boyette come out of her room with a
gun. Boyette raises it.

                    JULIET
          Shoot him!

Boyette aims it at Juliet instead.

                    JULIET
          Boyette...

                    BOYETTE
          Sit thee down.

The guards circle around to Juliet, guns drawn. Juliet sits
down on a chair.

Boyette walks up to the President who holds out his hand.
Boyette kisses his hand.

                    BOYETTE
          My complete master.

Juliet's face contorts in anger.

                    JULIET
          A kissing traitor! O serpent heart,
          hid with a flowering face! O that
          deceit should dwell in such a
          gorgeous palace! Turn thee, and
          look upon thy death.

Boyette looks down at the floor unable to handle the hate
Juliet now feels for her.


**INT. CAR - NAVARRE STREETS - DAY**

Romeo tries to call Juliet. Biron drives the BMW.


**INT. PRINCESS'S SUITE - DAY**

Juliet's phone rings. The President picks it up.

                    PRESIDENT
          What present hast thou here? Some
          certain treason.

The President sees the name on it. "ROMEO". Throws the phone
away and yells at Boyette.

                    PRESIDENT
          Hadst thou no poison mix'd?

Boyette works on filling up a SYRINGE with blue liquid.

The President moves to a corner bar and pours himself a
drink.

                    PRESIDENT
          Love. Ha. These violent delights
          have violent ends and in their
          triumph die, like fire and powder,
          which as they kiss consume.

Boyette bends down and whispers to Juliet.

> BOYETTE
> This distilled liquor, when through
> all thy veins shall run, no pulse,
> no warmth, no breath, shall testify
> thou livest; Each part, shall,
> stiff and stark and cold, appear
> like death: And in this borrow'd
> likeness of shrunk death, thou
> shalt continue until...

> JULIET
> Are you mad?

Boyette stabs Juliet with the syringe. Juliet looks at
Boyette as she loses her her ability to move or speak.

> BOYETTE
> Love is mad. The President, Romeo,
> I shall slay them both. Then will
> you be mine.

The President raises his glass and takes a sip and walks
over.

> PRESIDENT
> I'll watch her die.

The President leans in close to the Princess. He taps his
Phone.

> PRESIDENT
> Now, when Romeo comes, there art
> thou dead... a cup closed in thy
> hand... a dram of poison and drunk
> all. Then will Romeo come to his
> father.

The President kisses her. Boyette glares at him.

> PRESIDENT
> Thy lips are warm. For now.

Juliet struggles to keep her eyes open and hears his laugh
as she loses consciousness.

**EXT. SYCAMORE DAYS - DAY**

Romeo and Biron drive up.

**INT. SYCAMORE DAYS - NEAR ELEVATORS - DAY**

Romeo and Biron enter a stairwell and go to the elevator where the door is stuck trying to close against a leg. They enter the elevator.

**INT. ELEVATOR - DAY**

Romeo turns the body over. Its Rosaline. Biron hits a button and the elevator goes up.

>                    ROMEO
>           Rosaline...

**EXT. PRINCESS'S SUITE - DAY**

Romeo exits the elevator and finds TWO SOLDIERS armed to the hilt.

They stand down on seeing its Romeo and salute him.

**INT. PRINCESS'S SUITE - DAY**

Romeo enters to see Juliet on a chair. Eyes closed. Unmoving.

>                    ROMEO
>           Juliet!

He rushes to her. Checks her pulse.

Boyette sits on a chair in a dark corner.

>                    BOYETTE
>           Alas Poor Romeo. She is already
>           dead.

>                    ROMEO
>           Can heaven be so envious?

He turns back to Juliet.

>                    ROMEO
>           I will die with thee.

>                    PRESIDENT (O.S.)
>           No! My dear son!

Romeo sees the President rush into the room.

                    ROMEO
          Father!

                    PRESIDENT
          My child. My only life.

                    ROMEO
          Juliet, my only love. Here slain by
          my father. Is it even so? O, I am
          fortune's fool.

                    PRESIDENT
          No, no, not I. When I came, here
          untimely lay the noble Juliet dead.
          She, it seems did violence on
          herself. Look and thou shalt see.

The President points to the cup of poison.

In the dark corner, Boyette pulls out a gun.

In her hand, is the DISTINCTIVE GUN from the CEREMONIAL
CEREMONY seen in the beginning.

Something Romeo says makes her pause.

                    ROMEO
          Oh father. This means civil war.
          War, father. In that word's death.

                    PRESIDENT
          Be quiet.

                    ROMEO
          Death's the end of all.

                    PRESIDENT
          Be quiet. Or I'll make you quiet.

                    ROMEO
          Prevent the war, father. Bury your
          strife.

                    PRESIDENT
          Hang thee, disobedient wretch.
          Thursday, the civil war begins.

                    ROMEO
          And civil blood will make civil
          hands unclean. Good father, I
          beseech you on my knees...

                    BIRON
          Hear him with patience but to speak

a word.

                    PRESIDENT
          Flat treason 'gainst your
          President. Graze where you will,
          you shall not house with me.

The President SHOOTS Biron. Biron falls to the floor.

                    ROMEO
          No! Biron! Away to heaven,
          respective lenity. Fire-eyed fury
          be my conduct now.

The President feels the business end of a gun on the back of
his head.

Its Boyette. She puts her hand out for the President's gun.

                    PRESIDENT
               (to Boyette)
          Treason.

                    BOYETTE
          Nay, tyrant. Justice.

She takes the President's gun and throws it to Romeo.

                    BOYETTE
          Three words, dear Romeo. Deny thy
          father. You are a lover. Borrow
          Cupid's wings and soar with them
          above a common bound.

The President walks towards Romeo as he speaks.

                    PRESIDENT
          My son. She is a traitor. I am your
          father.

                    BOYETTE
          He is a tyrant. A murderer. For
          Juliet's sake, for Aquitaine's
          sake, strike him dead. Kill thy
          father. I hold it not a sin.

                    PRESIDENT
          Hold your tongue. Aquitaine is my
          crown jewel. Romeo is my son and
          thine enemy.

                    BOYETTE
          He is the end of all... the end of
          Juliet.

Boyette shows the SYRINGE with the blue liquid to Romeo.
Romeo looks to his father.

                    PRESIDENT
          Forgive me, Romeo.

The President pulls out a HIDDEN SNUB REVOLVER and shoots
Romeo.

                    ROMEO
          Shot, by heaven.

The President turns his gun on Boyette. He shoots and hits
her in the arm.

Her gun falls to the floor and she dives behind a sofa.

The President screams at both Boyette and Romeo as he walks
around the sofa.

                    PRESIDENT
          Look to't, think on't, I do not use
          to jest. Thursday is near; lay hand
          on heart, advise: An you be mine,
          I'll give you my all; And you be
          not, hang, beg, starve, die in the
          streets. For, by my soul, I'll
          ne'er acknowledge thee, Nor what is
          mine shall never do thee good.

                    ROMEO
          Villainous father. Their souls are
          but a little way above our heads,
          staying for thine to keep them
          company. Either thou, or I, or
          both, must go with them.

Romeo tries to rise, but fails.

The President aims at Boyette behind the sofa.

A SHOT rings out. The President falls.

Its Biron. Wounded. Holding Boyette's gun.

Boyette stands up. Biron aims the gun at her.

Boyette speaks to Romeo.

                    BOYETTE
          Thy Juliet is alive. I gave her a
          sleeping potion.

Boyette takes out a vial and waves it under Juliet's nose.

Juliet starts to stir.

Juliet opens her eyes.

Biron aims his gun at her.

                    BIRON
          Who are you?

Boyette doesn't answer.

                    JULIET
          Who are you?

                    BOYETTE
          I know not how to tell thee who I
          am. My name is an enemy to thee.

                    JULIET
          What is your name?

Boyette softly speaks her name, her slogan, her reason for
being.

                    BOYETTE
             Liberty.

Biron's face hardens. He walks over to her, and tears off
the sleeve of her right arm.

Then peels off the skin around her wrist, revealing a SKIN
TIGHT GLOW BAND, and a tattoo that reads "LIBERTY".

He holds it out for Juliet to see.

                    JULIET
          Our great enemy.

Juliet grabs the gun from Biron and aims at Boyette.

                    ROMEO
          No, Juliet.

Juliet turns to look at Romeo. With his last breath --

                    ROMEO
          Pardon her. Peace... in that
          word's... life.

He becomes very still.

                    JULIET
          Romeo...

She rushes over to him and checks his pulse. He's gone.

>              JULIET
>         Dead. For my life.

Biron walks up to his friend.

>              BIRON
>         Alas poor Romeo! Your wooing doth
>         not end like an old play. Jack hath
>         not Jill.


**EXT. DARK FIELDS - DAWN**

A BMW parked in the middle of a clearing in a wooded area.


**INT. CAR - DAWN**

Biron on the phone. Hangs up. He looks over to Boyette in
the passenger seat. She sits with a sad expression on her
face, her head hanging down.

>              BIRON
>         It is done. There will be no war.
>         A gentler judgment for you from
>         Queen Juliet. Not body's death, but
>         body's banishment from Navarre,
>         Verona and Aquitaine.

>              BOYETTE
>         Exiled from Aquitaine... Be
>         merciful, say 'death.'

>              BIRON
>         This is dear mercy, and thou seest
>         it not.

>              BOYETTE
>         'Tis torture, and not mercy.

>              BIRON
>         Boyette, arise. Do the thing I bid
>         thee do. Put not another sin on my
>         head. Fly hence. If ever you
>         disturb our streets again, your
>         life shall pay the forfeit of the
>         peace.

>              BOYETTE
>         I will be gone, sir, and not
>         trouble you.

Boyette steps out of the car and closes the door.

Juliet, sitting in the backseat, grits her teeth and gets out of the car and slams the door shut.

Biron remains inside the car.

**EXT. DESOLATE AREA - OUTSIDE THE CAR - NIGHT**

Boyette turns and looks at Juliet.

> JULIET
> Liberty. Our great enemy.

> BOYETTE
> It is so.

> JULIET
> How can this be true? You. A spy. I
> am much deceived.

> BOYETTE
> Truth is truth.

Boyette turns away. Then stops. Turns back.

> BOYETTE
> Juliet, you are... my only love
> sprung from only hate. Prodigious
> birth of love it is to me that I
> must love a loathed enemy.

> JULIET
> There's no trust, no faith, no
> honesty in you.

> BOYETTE
> (smiles sadly)
> Wilt thou leave me so unsatisfied?

> JULIET
> What satisfaction canst thou have
> tonight?

> BOYETTE
> A kiss? The exchange of thy love's
> faithful vow for mine?

> JULIET
> I give thee thy liberty. Go. While
> thou doth have night's cloak to
> hide thee.

>                         BOYETTE
>              Parting is such sweet sorrow.

Boyette glides away.

OUT OF THE SHADOWS, TWO ARMED MEN appear and they salute
Boyette.

>                       TWO ARMED MEN
>              Liberty!

Boyette and the two men disappear into the darkness.

Biron steps out of the car and looks at Juliet. She looks
back at him. They get back in the car and drive away.


**<u>THE END</u>**

# About the Author

Nikhil Kamkolkar is a writer-filmmaker and Unreal Authorized Instructor (Gold) blending story, cinematography, and real-time tech. An Unreal Engine Animation Fellowship alum, he works across development, previs, and final pixels, and is in pre-production on a sci-fi short that integrates Unreal with emerging AI workflows.

He wrote and directed the feature rom-com **LOVE LOVE** (streaming globally on Amazon Prime, HOOPLA, and more), plus award-winning shorts.

His TV pilots (sci-fi, horror, thriller) have placed in Screencraft and Final Draft Big Break. Alongside filmmaking, he's held day-job roles at Microsoft, MTV, Nickelodeon, and Topic. Several of his screenplays are published as books.

Based in New Jersey and working internationally, he focuses on filmmaker practice, creative resilience, and real-time/AI tooling.

❖

More at **KAM9.TV**.

❖

**Leave a Review**

If you liked reading this book, a short honest review really helps other creators discover it. Thank you.

# More From the Author

LOVE LOVE: Screenplay by Nikhil Kamkolkar (Rising Stakes Screenplay Series)

\*\*

Short Film Scripts: By Nikhil Kamkolkar (Rising Stakes Screenplay Series)

\*\*

RAW Deception: Novelization of a screenplay (Rising Stakes Screenplay Series)

\*\*

3 SHORT STORIES: Adapted from Short Film Screenplays (Rising Stakes Screenplay Series)

\*\*

LOVE LOVE: From Fantasy to Forever (Motion Picture)

Streaming on Amazon Prime, HOOPLA and others.

\*\*

LOVE LOVE: Fractures (Motion Picture)

Coming Soon

www.ingramcontent.com/pod-product-compliance
Lightning Source LLC
Chambersburg PA
CBHW041119120626

46547CB00019B/2778